Contents

KU-074-579

Preface

Colour blindness has been called the forgotten handicap. The common form of red-green colour deficiency is inherited and affects one out of every twelve men. Few women are colour-blind, about one in 200, yet nearly one in six women carries the gene that is responsible for the condition. It is typically passed on from a colour-blind grandfather, through his daughter, to a colour-blind grandson.

There is no cure and the condition is life long. Because the deficiency is permanent, the colour-blind person has no idea what they are missing. To them, the world appears normally coloured. There are bright colours and dull colours; some colours look pleasant, others less so. In fact, there is not the slightest reason to suspect that there is anything missing. Many colour-blind people remain unaware of their deficiency for years and only discover the true situation when refused entry to the career of their choice. I am colour-blind and have known it since a boy. It never seemed much of a handicap and at the age of seventeen I hopefully presented myself for flying training, thinking that I had a reasonable chance of passing the colour vision test if I tried hard enough. It turned out that I have the more severe type of colour blindness, as my eyes are completely lacking the type of receptor that is sensitive to red light. It was clear that several careers would be closed to me. I became a physicist. In the laboratory, there was always someone around to confirm whether I had wired up a mains plug correctly. It was only when doing research for this book that I came to realise just how much the colour-blind are missing, and just how little anyone else understands the condition. This book aims to provide a bridge between colour defectives and colour normals. It sets out to describe what the colour-blind see, to explore the consequences of defective colour vision and to give practical advice on dealing with some of the difficulties that may occur.

The first part of the book explains what colour is and how we see it. The eye focuses an image of the visual scene on the retina, which contains three types of photosensitive cones, sensitive to blue, green and red light. These correspond to the three primary colours and the sensation of colour that we experience is produced by the degree to which the three types of cone are stimulated. It is only man and the higher African apes that have three-colour vision. Almost all other mammals have two-colour vision, based on blue and green sensitive cones; some nocturnal mammals are totally colour-blind. In our terms, most mammals suffer from red-green colour blindness and so would have difficulty in spotting ripe fruit among the green leaves of a tree. The evidence is that three-colour vision in apes and man evolved relatively recently, too late to be found in the New World. The common red-green colour vision deficiencies result from the absence or alteration of either the red or green colour receptors. The resultant deficiency varies in type and severity. The most severely affected are known as dichromats and are completely lacking the red or green receptors. More commonly, one type of receptor is defective and the resultant deficiency can range from severe to very mild. While this book deals mostly with the common red-green deficiencies, other forms of colour blindness, such as achromatopsia (complete colour blindness), are also dealt with. It is also possible to acquire some forms of colour vision deficiency (abbreviated as CVD) in later life, as a result of illness or poisoning.

The second part of the book describes just what it is like to be colour-blind. Thanks to advances in computer manipulation of coloured images, it is possible to transform a coloured picture to show what the world looks like to a colour-blind person. Several examples are shown and will come as a surprise to parents, spouses and friends of the colour-blind. Unfortunately it is not possible to produce the reverse transformation. If only the colour-blind could be given a glimpse of what they are missing. The book does the next best thing and describes in words and diagrams the loss of sensation and the reduced ability to discriminate between colours. Using a device known as the chromaticity diagram, we show how most red-green defectives have difficulty in distinguishing between a range of colours running from green, through yellow and orange, to red. Not only that, but there is a shade of blue-green that is indistinguishable from grey.

Difficulties in seeing colours produce problems in everyday life. It is not just a matter of distinguishing traffic lights. Selecting food for quality and ripeness is difficult, as is any form of colour matching in decorating. A little-appreciated problem is the inability to appreciate skin colour. A blush or the pallor of ill-health go unnoticed, and a colour-blind husband may be accused of insensitivity to his wife's or children's appearance. A career as a fighter pilot or train driver is barred to the colour-blind, but CVD can produce unexpected difficulties in a wide range of occupations. Even an apparently risk-free profession as accountancy has pitfalls for the colour-blind, where the failure to notice that an account is literally in the red can result in an expensive mistake. This book lists careers where CVD may be a barrier to entry, or where difficulties may arise in practice.

Quack cures for colour blindness were peddled in the last century to those hoping to fly in the Air Force, but produced no benefit at all. Inherited colour vision deficiency is in the genes and nothing can be done about it. However, it is possible to use aids to assist with colour discrimination. The use of tinted glasses can enable the colour defective to discriminate between colours that would normally be indistinguishable. One technique uses a tinted spectacle lens or contact lens over one eye only. Colour discrimination is improved and the rivalry between the two eyes produces a sensation of colour brightness. There is no way that such aids can produce true colour vision, but there are many enthusiastic wearers.

While writing this book I have come into contact with many people doing research into colour vision and colour vision deficiencies. It is an active field, especially since advances in genetics have enabled the genes for colour vision to be studied in detail. There is now a very good understanding of the nature of the genetic defects that result in colour vision deficiency. It is possible to carry out a blood test that will precisely diagnose the nature and severity of any deficiency. Another important advance has been the development of computer based techniques that simulate the appearance of the world as seen by the colour deficient. The contents of this book cover the most recent developments.

Donald McIntyre
Chester, 2002

PART 1

The Causes of Colour Blindness

Chapter 1 - Light and colour

In 1665 Cambridge University was closed by the Great Plague. Isaac Newton, yet to become England's most famous scientist, had to return home after his graduation. In a remarkable two years, he produced the binomial theorem and the foundations of calculus in mathematics, the theory of gravity and the basic understanding of colour. In his own words *"for in those days I was in the prime of my age for invention"*.

It was well known at the time that passing white light through a prism produced a spectrum of colours similar to that seen in a rainbow, but it was generally believed that the glass in the prism in some way modified the light, turning white rays into coloured rays. It was Newton's genius to show that white light consists of a mixture of colours and that the action of the prism was to split the light into its constituent parts. White light consists of a mixture of colours, which are bent, or refracted, through different angles as they enter and leave the prism; red rays are bent the least and blue the most. This was confirmed by Newton's observation that a single colour could not be persuaded to produce any other colour by passing it though further prisms, and by showing that white light could be reconstituted by combining the colours of the spectrum together. Newton was also percipient enough to realise that the sensation of colour lies within our eyes and brains: *"rays, to speak properly, are not coloured. In them there is nothing else than a certain power . . . to stir up a sensation of this or that colour"*.

The spread of colour produced by a prism or by a rainbow is termed the **spectrum**, running from red to blue. Newton considered it to consist of seven primary colours, and his terminology has been preserved as the conventional naming of the colours of the rainbow. His choice of seven subdivisions was influenced by his interest in the science of music. The musical scale of one octave contains seven full tones and Newton accordingly divided the visible spectrum into seven equal parts, a number that also had mystical connotations. Newton's seven colours of the spectrum were red, orange, yellow, green, blue, indigo, violet. The names may be recalled using the old mnemonic *Richard Of York Gave Battle In Vain* or its playground equivalent *Run Off You Girls, Boys In View*. There was a bit of wishful thinking on Newton's part when he managed to fit in seven colours; few people would reliably claim to be able to distinguish between blue, indigo and violet in a rainbow. The spectrum is shown in *Figure 1* (see page 65), which shows the more commonly used modern names. The boundaries separating the colours are not exactly defined; typical values are shown.

Newton's concept of seven primary colours has no basis either in physics or physiology. He conceived light as consisting of a flux of seven sizes of particles, corresponding to the seven rainbow colours. When the behaviour of light is studied in the science laboratory, it exhibits characteristics of both a wave motion and of a stream of particles, the so-called wave-particle duality. For many physical and chemical phenomena, it is advantageous to consider light as consisting of a stream of small packets of energy, termed **photons**. The energy of a photon is related to the wavelength of the light. Blue photons are more energetic than red, which explains why blue light is more effective at causing physical and chemical changes, such as the fading of dyes in fabrics or pigments in pictures. Ultra-violet light, while invisible to the eye, is more energetic still and is the part of sunlight responsible for causing sunburn.

However, most colour-related phenomena are best considered in terms of the wave nature of light. Visible light is a form of electromagnetic radiation. Other forms include X rays, microwaves and radio waves. All these types of radiation move through space, travelling in straight lines and moving at the speed of light. The type of radiation may be precisely described by its **wavelength.** The wavelength of light is very small indeed and is less than the smallest distance that may be seen with an optical microscope. There is no need to visualise the microscopic distance corresponding to the wavelength; consider it simply as a number that gives an unambiguous measure of the colour of the light. The unit for wavelength adopted in this book is the **nanometre**, abbreviated to nm, which is a length of one billionth of a metre. The visible spectrum covers the range from 400 to 700 nm. Wavelengths somewhat longer than 700 nm may just be visible as a very deep red, but 700 nm serves as a practical limit. The wavelengths have been added to the spectrum in Figure 1.

Light sources

All solid surfaces emit radiation and the higher the temperature, the shorter the wavelength. Even the warm surface of a human body gives off long wave infrared radiation. The wavelength is far too long to be seen by the eye, but the radiation can be detected with a specialised thermal imaging camera. Raising the temperature of an object, such as a piece of iron in a blacksmith's forge, will both increase the amount of radiated energy and shorten its wavelength. At a temperature of about $600\,^{\circ}C$, the iron begins to glow with a dull red; as the temperature increases the iron glows brighter, changing through bright red and orange at around 1700°C to reach a yellow-white heat at a temperature of 3000°C. The surface of the sun has a temperature of 5000°C; evolution has ensured that the response of the human eye is well matched to the light received from the sun. About half of the sun's energy is concentrated into the narrow spectral range visible to the eye, and the peak energy density of solar radiation occurs at a wavelength of 470 nm; this is close to the region of maximal sensitivity of the eye, which occurs at 550 nm.

The colour of an object as we see it depends on the mixture of light wavelengths that leave the surface and reach the eye. This mixture depends in turn on the wavelength composition of the light that illuminates the object and the true colour of the surface. The true colour is the colour appearance when the surface is illuminated by white light. Needless to say, there are now several international standards defining just what white light is. The subtleties need not concern us; the light produced by an overcast sky provides an adequate example. An illuminating light source that does not contain all the wavelengths of white light cannot show objects in their true colour. The most obvious example of this is the extreme colour distortions seen under a yellow sodium street lamp; the colours look terrible even to a colour defective. *Figure 2* compares the spectra of sunlight, a domestic light bulb and a fluorescent lamp. The fluorescent lamp produces an uneven distribution of wavelengths, which may produce unexpected effects on the colour appearance of some objects.

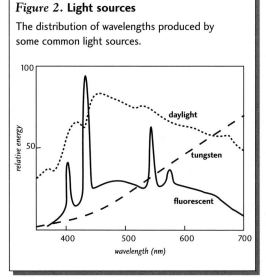

Figure 2. Light sources
The distribution of wavelengths produced by some common light sources.

For some purposes, it is necessary to know how a light source affects colour appearance. There are two important properties:

- The colour appearance of a source describes how "warm" or "cool" it appears. It is described by the colour temperature of the source. By convention, colour temperatures are always expressed in degrees Kelvin. A temperature in degrees Kelvin is equal to the Celsius temperature plus 273.

- The colour rendering properties of a light source indicate how well colours can be seen under the light, compared with ideal white light.

The expressions 'warm' and 'cool' are used to describe the appearance of colours and light sources. Our human experience is to associate red and orange with firelight and hot coals and these colours are thought of as warm. Conversely, bluish light is described as cool. These descriptive terms are the opposite way round from the more technical idea of colour temperature. A red light source has a lower colour temperature than a blue source.

The eye and brain between them are remarkably good at automatically adjusting for the effects of different light sources on the colour appearance of a scene. For instance, a familiar room interior does not appear very different whether seen in daylight or by artificial light. The eye compensates for the difference between the colour temperatures of daylight and artificial light. Photographic film is not so forgiving. For accurate colour photography it is necessary to maintain the correct balance between film type and the type of lamp or flash used. Photographic light sources and films are characterised by their colour temperature; if they do not match, it will be necessary to use correction filters.

Colour rendering of a light source is measured as the **colour rendering index**, where the highest score of 100 is given to an ideal source. For convenience, lamps may be classified into colour rendering groups, which are set out in *Table 1*.

Table 1. **CIE colour rendering index and applications**

CIE Colour Rendering Group	Colour Rendering Index	Application
1A	100 - 91	where accurate colour matching is required, e.g. colour printing inspection
1B	90 - 81	where good colour rendering is required, e.g. some shops and other commercial premises
2	80-61	where moderate colour rendering is acceptable
3	60 - 41	where colour rendering is of little significance but marked distortion of colour is unacceptable
4	40 - 20	where colour rendering is of no importance

Table 2 lists various light sources and their characteristics, which should be taken as an approximate guide only. Lamps are produced in a wide variety of types for different applications; the same class of lamp may often be obtained with a range of colour rendering groups. Where colour rendering is important it is necessary to check the colour rendering class of the lamp from manufacturer's data. The type of lamp used will affect the results of a colour vision test. The standard tests all specify the type of illumination that should be used.

Table 2. Light Sources

Light source	Colour appearance	Colour temperature (K)	Colour rendering
Overcast sky	North light	7000	
Noon sun		5500	
Fluorescent	Cool	4000	1A to 3
Fluorescent	Intermediate	3500	1B to 3
Fluorescent	Warm	3000	1A to 3
GLS filament (light bulb)		2700	1A
Tungsten halogen		3000	1A
High pressure mercury		3500	3
Low pressure sodium	Monochromatic yellow	-	poor
High pressure sodium	Warm yellow	2500	2

Reflection and transmission

Consider a beam of white light falling on a solid object - say a piece of coloured plastic. The white light consists of a mixture of wavelengths, i.e. a mixture of different colours. What happens to the light as it reaches the object depends on the wavelength of the light and the material constituting the object. For each colour

- some is reflected
- some is transmitted and emerges from the far side of the object
- some is absorbed inside the object, where it turns into heat and is never seen again

An opaque object that appears red when illuminated by white light does so because colours other than red have been absorbed, leaving only the red wavelengths to be reflected. A transparent piece of glass that allows red and green wavelengths to pass through but absorbs all blue, will be seen as yellow, *Figure 3*.

Figure 3. **Transmission and reflection**

Solid and transparent colours.
(a) An opaque red surface absorbs all colours other than red.
(b) A yellow filter absorbs blue light and passes red and green.

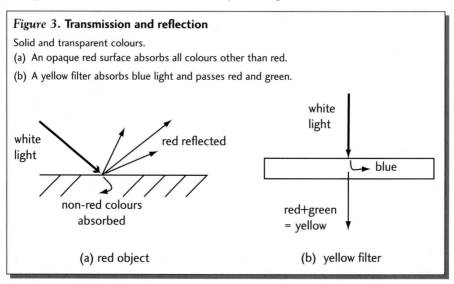

A white material has a high and equal reflectance to all wavelengths; white paper has a reflectance of around 85%. Grey surfaces have a lower reflectance, which is the same or similar for all visible wavelengths. Pure black is rarely encountered; if it were, it would not be possible to see the object, but only deduce that something was there by the absence of anything visible. Black paper may have a reflectance as low as 4%. Black velvet is the blackest material, traditionally used by photographers and conjurers

Colours may be produced in other ways. A very thin soap film shows **interference colours**; this is caused by a phenomenon that is explicable on the wave nature of light and is much loved by physics teachers. Such colours are often to be seen when viewing a thin film of oil on the surface of water. A similar phenomenon is also responsible for the metallic lustre appearance of some animals, such as beetles and fish, where it is known as **iridescence.**

Colour mixing

It is impossible to discuss the physics of colour and colour mixing without some understanding of the eye. The physiology of the eye and the psychology of perception are presented more fully in later chapters. For the moment, the following summary of colour perception will assist in an understanding of colour mixing.

- The part of the retina concerned with colour perception contains three types of light sensitive receptors, sensitive to red, green and blue light.

- Coloured light falling on the retina excites the three types of receptor to different degrees, according to its colour. The nervous system and brain interpret the combination of signals from the receptors as a colour.

- A combination of two or more coloured lights entering the eye is interpreted as a single colour. The brain is incapable of distinguishing the components of a colour mixture. The eye differs from the ear in this respect, since the ear is capable of separating the components of a musical chord.

Colours can be mixed to produce a colour different from any of the component parts of the mixture. If coloured lights are mixed so that they all enter the eye together, say by projecting several colours so that they overlap on a white screen, the process is known as additive mixing. When coloured paints or pigments are mixed, as on an artist's palette, the process is termed subtractive mixing. The reasons for these terms will become clear.

Additive mixing

The classic demonstration of additive colour mixing is shown in *Figure 4* (see page 65). Red, green and blue lights are shone on a white surface. The colours produced by mixing may be summarised:

Table 3. **Additive colour mixing**

Primaries are red, green and blue

Components	Result
Red + Green + Blue	White
Red + Green	Yellow
Red + Blue	Magenta (bluish red)
Green + Blue	Cyan (greenish blue)

Yellow, magenta and cyan are known as the **additive secondaries.** The colour terms cyan and magenta, while not common in everyday speech, are important in the world of colour vision and colour reproduction. The names are of recent origin; magenta was named after the blood spilled at the battle of Magenta in 1859. Almost any colour found in the world may be reproduced by the additive mixture of three primaries. The reservation "almost" applies to some surface effects, like a metallic sheen, and some strong pure colours. Note that the colour mixing takes place in the eye and brain. If red and green are mixed, the red and green rays of light stay entirely independent of each other on the way into the eye, where they separately stimulate the different types of cone in different proportions. It is the brain that interprets the results as a sensation of yellow. There is no unique definition of the three additive primary colours. The most effective choice of primaries are well separated in the visual spectrum and in fact do not coincide with the peak sensitivities of the cones in the eye.

Subtractive mixing

When a coloured paint is illuminated by white light, it reflects some wavelengths and absorbs the rest. When two paints are mixed together, the only colours reflected by the mixture are those which are absorbed by neither of the constituents. The appearance of the mixture is the colour that is left after each part of the mixture has subtracted the absorbed colours from the incident white light. The rules of subtractive colour mixing are therefore the opposite of those for additive mixing.

Table 4. Subtractive colour mixing

Primaries are yellow, magenta and cyan

Colours	Result
Yellow + Magenta + Cyan	Black
Yellow + Magenta	Red
Yellow + Cyan	Green
Magenta + Cyan	Blue

Thus, mixing yellow and cyan paints results in green. The yellow paint on its own reflects red and green, but absorbs blue. The cyan paint reflects green and blue, but absorbs red. The mixture absorbs both red and blue, leaving only the green to be reflected. Subtractive mixing depends on the coloured paints being impure and reflecting a broad range of wavelengths. If it were possible to obtain pure spectral paints, then mixing any two different colours would produce black.

Subtractive mixing is used in colour printing. The usual process uses transparent yellow, cyan and magenta inks. Combining colours is done by overprinting, rather than mixing. This process will reproduce most colours, but does not give a satisfactory black and an additional black ink is normally used, to give the so-called four-colour process, referred to as CMYK. Television uses a form of additive mixing known as **partitive**. The components of the colour mix are in form of small dots of colour placed side by side. Physically, these consist of dots of three types of phosphor deposited on the inner surface of the TV screen. When excited by the scanning beam of electrons that recreates the TV image, each phosphor dot glows in one of the primary colours. The eye is unable to resolve adjacent dots or pixels spatially and the result is an additive mix.

Colour theories and wheels

Since Newton's time, there have been many theories of colour, which have attempted to rationalise the subjective experience that some colours appear to harmonise with each other, while others clash or contrast unpleasantly. One aim has been to produce rules for the use of colour by artists and designers that will help in the composition of a pleasing picture. Most expositions of harmony and contrast have involved placing colours in sequence round the circumference of a wheel. Red and blue are at opposite ends of the spectrum. However, it seems intuitive that as one moves beyond blue and violet, it is only a short step to get back to red via a linking colour of purple. Purple is a non-spectral colour and cannot be imitated by light of a single wavelength; the sensation is produced from the simultaneous excitation of red and blue cones by a mixture of colours.

Figure 5 (see page 65) shows a simple colour wheel, based on the principles of additive colour mixing. The wheel may be built up step by step. Start by placing the three primaries red, green and blue at equidistant positions round the rim of the wheel. The respective complementaries are placed opposite the primaries. Mixing opposite colours additively produces white light.

Classification of colour

The names of colours used in everyday speech are imprecise. Speakers may not agree on the exact meaning of a colour name, and colour names do not translate unambiguously between different languages. There have been many proposals for a standardised colour specification. The one most widely used was introduced by an artist, Albert Munsell, at the beginning of the twentieth century. He divided the colour appearance of a surface into three independent variables:

- **Hue** is the fundamental colour, e.g. red, purple, green. Munsell followed the practice of the colour theorists in arranging the colours in a circle.

- **Chroma (or saturation)** describes the purity of the colour on a range running from pure colour to a grey of the same value. As the saturation decreases, the amount of white light diluting the colour increases.

- **Value (or lightness)** covers the range from light to dark on a scale running from black to white.

The Munsell scale uses 10 hues, derived from 5 basic colour names and their intermediates. The complete Munsell scale is arranged as a three-dimensional solid, known as the surface-colour perception solid, *Figure 6* (see page 66). The central, vertical axis represents the greys, running from black at the bottom to white at the top. The hues are arranged in a circle round the central axis and the horizontal distance from the axis represents the degree of saturation. A colour is specified as H V/C, where H is the hue, V the value and C the chroma. Sample colours are published as the Munsell Book of Colour.

The Munsell scale is designed for the classification of paints and dyes. Different words, but with closely similar meanings, are sometimes used when talking about luminous sources, e.g. lights instead of materials. This book will stick to the terms **hue, saturation** and **lightness.** While not Munsell's original terminology, the **HSL** system is used in several computer graphic systems and so is likely to be familiar to many people. Typically, the hue is set to a number running from 1 to 256, which is more than the average eye can reliably distinguish.

The most effective way of showing the relationship between different colours is by using the **CIE chromaticity diagram**. This diagram has been used for years as a fundamental tool by experts in the fields of colour technology and lighting design, but is otherwise little known outside this specialist field. The diagram allows the colour that results when mixing two, three or more colours in varying proportions to be predicted by means of a simple geometrical construction. Of particular interest to readers of this book is the ability of the chromaticity diagram to predict the colour confusions experienced by colour defectives. For this reason, discussion of the chromaticity diagram has been postponed until Chapter 4.

Colour names

One of the aims of this book is to improve communication between those with colour vision deficiency and those with normal vision. Language is our prime means of communication; indeed many philosophers hold that language enables, determines and ultimately restricts our thinking. The technical ways in which colours can be classified and named have been discussed above. However, these are not the names used in common speech and it is worth looking at the way in which different civilisations throughout history and over the world have named colours. There have been several attempts to produce dictionaries of colour, in which colours are described verbally. One such example ran:

> Puce. A dark red that is yellower and less strong than cranberry, paler and slightly yellower than average garnet, blue, less strong and slightly lighter than pomegranate, and bluer and paler than average wine

Descriptions such as this are surely of no help to anyone, whether colour defective or not.

It turns out that early societies paid remarkably little attention to the abstract concept of colour. William Gladstone, who was a classical scholar as well as Prime Minister of Great Britain in the nineteenth century, analysed Greek literature for the usage of colour terms. He concluded that the Greeks probably had defective colour vision, since they used so few colour descriptive words. Most of the colour references in Homer's epic poem *The Iliad* are just to light and dark, with blue not getting a mention at all. Gladstone concluded that by the nineteenth century the "organ of colour" had become more highly developed in civilised peoples. In the spirit of the times, when the British Empire was at its peak, he stated the British had *"some special aptitude in this respect, as we may judge from the comparatively advantageous position which the British painters have always held as colourists among other contemporary schools."*

The use of colour names is by no means consistent in different cultures and societies. Many cultures employ an extensive vocabulary to classify the appearance of objects that have importance to the workings of that society. East Africans have a wide range of precise terms to describe the appearance of cattle, as the English do for horses: consider *strawberry, roan, piebald, skewbald, chestnut, bay.* The Inuit have a wide vocabulary for subtle variations in the appearance of ice and snow, though not the several hundred sometimes attributed to them. A language spoken in the Philippines confounds concepts of succulence with that of colour, so that the descriptive words combine concepts of moistness, freshness, dried up, etc., with those for green and brown. Thus, many of the words used in such societies are not pure colour terms but remain attached to the object that they describe; they cannot be used, for instance, to name the colour of a light source projected on a screen. Indeed, some of the languages contain no word for the concept of colour. A Danish anthropologist landing on a Polynesian island with a set of standard Munsell colours was greeted with the words *"We don't talk much about colour here"*.

If descriptive words that are linked to the appearance of a restricted class of objects are excluded, what pure colour terms are left? The fundamental study to deal with this was carried out some years ago by two American anthropologists, Brent Berlin and Paul Kay. They investigated basic colour terms in nearly 100 languages over the world. They defined "basic colour term" to exclude description of objects, aiming at an abstract concept that could be applied to any coloured stimulus. The criteria for a colour name to qualify as a basic colour term were

- The word must be simple. Composite words, e.g. honey-coloured or reddish-brown, would be excluded.

- It should be a Level 1 word, by which Berlin and Kay meant that the word should stand on its own and not be included in another Level 1 word. For instance, red is a Level 1 word. Scarlet, vermilion, crimson etc. are classed as level 2 words, since they are all included in the overall concept of red.

- The meaning must be clear and the word in common use. This excludes such terms as cyan, which is precise, but is not used in everyday speech.

- The use of the word must not be restricted to particular contexts or objects.

Berlin and Kay found that all natural languages have between 2 and eleven basic colour terms. They also found that where a language had a restricted set of words, only certain combinations of colour terms were found. This can be interpreted as a sequence of evolutionary changes. The first colour terms to appear are black and white; every language has these. The next term to be added is red, followed by either green or yellow. When green and yellow have been added, blue and brown appear in sequence. The final stage is to add purple, pink, orange and grey in any order. While subsequent studies have found minor qualifications to Berlin and Kay's rules, the general picture stays remarkably intact.

Table 5. **Stages in language development**	
Stage	**Colours added**
1	White, Black
2	Red
3	Green or Yellow
4	Yellow or Green
5	Blue
6	Brown
7	Purple, Pink, Orange, Grey

There are exceptions, and not all modern languages contain all the basic colour terms. Welsh has no word that directly translates the basic colour terms of green, blue, grey and brown; instead it has three words with somewhat different colour boundaries. On the other hand, Russian does not have a word for blue, but instead has two words, roughly translated as light blue and dark blue, which are regarded as distinct colours. Nearer to home, the French do not have an equivalent general purpose word for brown; the several words for brown are related to different classes of objects.

Summary: Light

Light is the visible part of the electromagnetic spectrum, which includes other forms of radiation such as radio waves and X-rays. White light is made up of a mixture of all visible colours, which together constitute the visible spectrum. A pure spectral colour is defined by its wavelength, which is measured in nanometres (nm). The eye can see wavelengths from 400 nm (violet) to 700 nm (red).

Coloured light emitted by a source or reflected from an object consists of a mixture of wavelengths. The eye and brain between them combine the wavelengths to produce the sensation of a single colour. When coloured lights are combined, the eye sees a new single colour, not a mixture of colours. The process is known as additive mixing. In contrast, the mixing of paints is known as subtractive mixing, since each added paint removes wavelengths from the reflected light. The additive primary colours are red, green and blue, which mixed together in equal proportions produce the sensation of white light. Nearly all colours visible to the eye can be produced by mixing the three primary colours in different proportions.

There is a wide variety of natural and artificial light sources. Each produces its own mixture of light wavelengths and the appearance of objects illuminated by a source depends on this mixture. Artificial light sources are categorised by a colour rendering index, to indicate how good they are at revealing true colours.

There are several systems of classifying colours. The most widely used is the Munsell system, which describes a colour in terms of three variables, hue saturation and lightness.

- Hue is the fundamental colour, e.g. red, blue, green, etc.

- Saturation measures the purity of the colour; a desaturated colour is diluted with white light.

- Lightness is simply the brightness of the colour, running from dark to light.

Chapter 2 - Colour vision

The eye is our most important sensory organ and this is reflected in the substantial proportion of the brain that is devoted to vision. The old saying that a picture is worth a thousand words if anything understates the case. Those who have started manipulating photographs on a computer soon realise that the amount of storage space used up by a simple picture file is vastly greater than that occupied by a word processor file. This chapter describes the working of the eye and how it deals with the wavelengths contained in light to produce the sensation we know as colour.

The eye

The structure of the human eye is shown in *Figure 7* (see page 66). The lens forms an image of the scene being viewed on the rear surface of the eyeball, in the same way as a camera focuses an image on the film. The equivalent of the camera film in the eye is the **retina**, which is a complex layer covering inside surface of the rear of the eyeball. It contains the light sensitive cells that detect light and colour, plus some very complicated interconnections between various nervous pathways. We will not describe the lens and optical behaviour of the eye in any detail, but concentrate on the way in which the retina detects the light and eventually produces a colour sensation. There is a distinction to be made here between colour sensation and colour perception. Sensation deals with colours in isolation; an experimental psychologist studying colour vision may use coloured light projected onto a white screen, with no relation to an actual object. Perception deals with the way the brain interprets what the eye sees. When a real scene is viewed, the brain adds some extra interpretation based on experience and expectation. This can produce situations where the brain misinterprets actuality, creating optical illusions. First we discuss the eye and the mechanism of colour sensation.

Photoreceptors and photopigments
The light sensitive cells or **photoreceptors** are situated at the rear surface of the retina and the incoming light has to pass through a transparent layer of nerve cells before reaching them. This arrangement is hardly efficient; only about 20% of the photons entering the eye get absorbed by the photoreceptors. However, the receptors are extremely sensitive. Under the most favourable conditions, only a few photons are required to produce a sensation of light in the eye. The photoreceptors

are of two types, **rods** and **cones**, so called because of their shape. Cones are employed for accurate vision in bright light, in detail and in colour. When we look directly at something of interest, the image falls in the centre of the retina, and that is where the cones have their highest concentration. The diameter of the smallest cone is about 1 micron, only twice the wavelength of light, and there is a total of some 6 million cones in all. Cones are distributed over the central area of the retina known as the **macula**, which covers an area of about 1 x 3 mm, with the longer dimension roughly horizontal. The image of the part of the scene that the eye is concentrating on falls on the **fovea**. This is a small area of the macula, about one quarter of a millimetre in diameter and containing about 100,000 cones tightly packed together. The rods are less densely packed and are to be found mostly in the outer regions of the retina. There is a total of 120 million rods. The rods have no ability to discriminate colours and are at their most sensitive in dim light. Daylight dazzles the rods and they become insensitive; when we move from light into darkness it takes the rods about 30 minutes to become dark adapted and achieve maximum sensitivity. People used to working in very low light levels learn the trick of looking slightly away from the object of interest, so that the image falls on the sensitive rods outside the central region and not on the less sensitive cones in the fovea. Astronomers using an optical telescope learn to 'look off' when observing faint stars.

The rods and cones contain light sensitive chemicals known as **photopigments**. When light is absorbed in a photoreceptor it causes a chemical change in the photopigment; this gives rise to an electrical signal that is conducted via a network of nervous connections within the thickness of the retina to the optic nerve, which sends the signals off to the brain.

There are four types of photopigment: one found in the rods and the other three associated with the three types of cone. **Rhodopsin** is the photopigment found in rods. It is also known as visual purple because of its colour. When the rods are exposed to bright light, the rhodopsin bleaches; after a period of darkness, it returns to its former colour. **Cone pigments** are of three types, which are sensitive to different regions of the colour spectrum. The photochemical behaviour is similar to that of rhodopsin; the pigment is bleached on exposure to light, though the cone pigments recover much faster than rhodopsin. The cone photopigments have proved much harder to study than the rhodopsin found in rods. It has been shown that about 40% of their structure is held in common with that of rhodopsin. However, the red and green photopigments are chemically very similar to each other and share about 90% of their structure. This supports the theory that the red and green receptors have a common origin in the relatively recent evolutionary past.

Scotopic vision

At low light levels, corresponding to a moonlit landscape or darker, the light reaching the retina is too dim to stimulate cone vision and seeing takes place using the rods only. On moving from light to darkness, the rods become steadily more sensitive as the eye adapts to darkness. Maximum sensitivity is reached in about 30 minutes, when vision is said to be **scotopic.** In this condition the rods are very sensitive indeed and a rod can respond to the incidence of a single photon of light. The spectral sensitivity of a rod is shown in Figure 8, where it can be seen that peak sensitivity occurs at a wavelength of about 500 nm. The dark-adapted eye is maximally sensitive to blue-green light and quite insensitive to red light. While dark adaptation takes half an hour to establish fully, it is lost immediately on exposure to bright light. It is a chemical phenomenon, governed by the rates of bleaching and regeneration of rhodopsin, rather than a process occurring in the brain. When both eyes are fully dark adapted, try exposing one to light while keeping the other tight shut. Return to dim light and one eye will retain its adaptation and ability to see, while the one exposed to light will be virtually blind.

Rod vision is colour-blind. Figure 8 shows that the rods are sensitive to a range of colours. Light falling on a rod produces a signal whose strength indicates only the quantity of light that has fallen on the rod in the recent past, about the last tenth of a second or so. The response curve shows that the rod will produce the same signal from a given amount of light with a wavelength of 500 nm as it would do from twice that amount of light with a wavelength of 550 nm. In consequence, rods have no way of distinguishing between the two situations and the brain does not respond with any sensation of colour.

Photopic vision

Normal vision is classed as **photopic vision,** when the three types of cones are active, providing acute vision for the seeing of detail and also colour vision. Photopic vision, which includes colour vision, takes place over a very wide range of brightness, from bright sunlight to indoors on a dull day. We can plot the spectral sensitivity of the light adapted eye in a similar manner to that of the dark adapted and the two are compared in *Figure 8*. This plots the overall sensation of brightness and ignores colour sensation. To produce these curves, subjects are asked to compare the brightnesses of lights of different colours. This can be done using an instrument known as the flicker photometer, where the two colours are presented in rapid succession and their relative strengths adjusted until they appear equal. The flicker makes it possible to compare the brightnesses of the two lights without being confused by the difference in colour. The photopic sensitivity curve is of considerable technical importance to lighting engineers and has been standardised by the relevant international authority, when it is known as the CIE V_λ Curve. The curve shows that the light adapted eye is more sensitive towards the red end

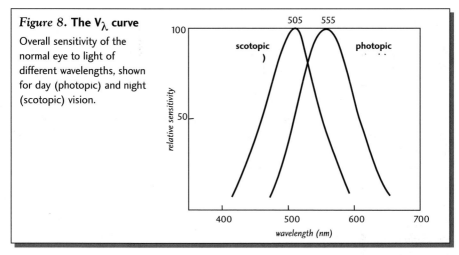

Figure 8. The V$_\lambda$ curve

Overall sensitivity of the normal eye to light of different wavelengths, shown for day (photopic) and night (scotopic) vision.

of the spectrum than is the dark adapted eye. Peak sensitivity occurs at 555 nm for photopic vision and at 505 for scotopic. This change in wavelength is known as the Purkinje shift, after its discoverer. Jan Purkinje was a pioneering Czech physiologist and friend of Goethe, whose other discoveries included the use of fingerprints for identification. The effects of the Purkinje shift may be observed for yourself. As the light fades in the evening, the relative brightness of flowers in a garden changes; the reds become much darker or black, while the blues become brighter. As the light fails, rod vision begins to take over from cone vision; the rods are unable to detect reds, so the red flowers darken faster than the blue.

Three - colour vision

Newton's demonstration that white light is composed of all the spectral colours left unresolved the problem of how these colours are received and experienced by the eye and brain. Why do we see only a single colour when two coloured lights are mixed, and not the visual equivalent of the chord heard when two notes are played simultaneously? If there were many types of receptor, each capable of responding to a particular coloured wavelength, then monochromatic light would appear much dimmer than white light, since the single wavelength would not stimulate the other receptors. This problem was tackled successfully for the first time by Thomas Young in the early part of the nineteenth century. Young was an English physician and physicist who carried out the experiments that demonstrated conclusively that light behaved as a wave motion. He had many other interests; he played a prominent part in the decipherment of the Rosetta stone, the ancient stone text that provided the key to deciphering Egyptian hieroglyphs. Young proposed that the eye contained a limited number of different colour receptors and supposed that there were three "principal colours, red, yellow and blue", which he later changed to red, green and violet. Unfortunately, Young's work was disparaged at the time by most English scientists, as any opposition to a theory of Newton's was unthinkable. It required the support of French physicists to achieve acceptance of the wave theory of light, and of the German physicist Hermann L.F. von Helmholtz to develop the theory of colour, which became known as the Young-Helmholtz three-colour theory. Young's contribution to the theory of colour vision is fundamental and was summarised by the scientist James Clerk Maxwell in the words:

> *"It seems a truism to say that colour is a sensation; and yet Young, by honestly recognising this elementary truth, established the first consistent theory of colour. So far as I know, Thomas Young was the first who, starting from the well-known fact that there are three primary colours, sought for the explanation of this fact, not in the nature of light but in the nature of man".*

The three types of cone are not uniformly distributed over the retina. By using a very narrow beam of light, only about 2 microns across, it is possible to measure the absorption of individual cones and so determine their nature. It turns out that the blue cones account for only about 3% of the total number of cone photoreceptors. It would seem that the red and green photoreceptors do most of the work for fine vision and the seeing of detail, shapes and movement. There is a plausible explanation for this arrangement. The simple optical arrangement of the eye suffers from chromatic aberration. Just as Newton's prism bent different colours by different amounts, so does the lens of the eye. The consequence is that it is impossible to focus the blue and red regions of a multicoloured object simultaneously; one or other will be out of focus. Camera lenses have a sophisticated design, using several components made of different types of glass to overcome this problem. The lens of the eye is crude in comparison. It would seem, then, that the red and green cones, which operate at very similar wavelengths, provide detailed information to the brain, while the out of focus blue component of the image is used to colour-in the picture.

The spectral response curves of the three types of cones are shown in **Figure 9**. The scientific literature refers to the cones as L, M and S, standing for Long, Medium and Short wave receptors. We shall continue to refer to them as red, green and blue cones, though it is evident from the figure that the "red" cone is at its most sensitive to light with a wavelength around 565 nm, which is yellow. Note also that there is a great deal of overlap in the curves; indeed, any wavelength between 400 and 500 nm will excite all three cones and any wavelength between 400 and 650 nm will excite at least two cones. It is the relative response of the three types of cones that the brain interprets as colour.

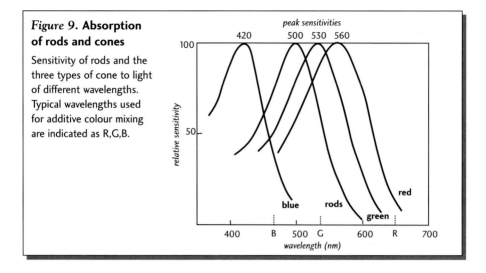

Figure 9. Absorption of rods and cones

Sensitivity of rods and the three types of cone to light of different wavelengths. Typical wavelengths used for additive colour mixing are indicated as R,G,B.

The three sensitivity curves are fundamental to the understanding of colour vision. The brain uses the signals from the three sets of cones to interpret both the brightness and the colour of the incoming light. Colour depends on the relative strengths of the signals from the cones. Consider, for instance, how sensitive the eye is to a change in wavelength of the incoming light. Light with a wavelength of 700 nm is at the practical limit of vision; any longer wavelength and it would be invisible and classed as infrared. Light of this wavelength excites only the red cones and with a low efficiency at that: just one twentieth of that for the most sensitive region in the yellow. If the wavelength of the light is shortened towards 650 nm, the red cones rapidly become more sensitive. However, there is little change in the response of the green cones, which are very insensitive in this region. The brain therefore interprets the wavelength change as an increase in brightness of the light, with little change in colour. In contrast, round about a wavelength of 500 nm, a change in wavelength of incoming monochromatic light produces a rapid change in the response of all three types of cone. The eye is capable of very fine colour discrimination in this region. The difference in wavelength between two colours that can just be distinguished by the eye is termed the discrimination and is shown as a function of wavelength in **Figure 10**. As would be expected, discrimination is poorest at the two ends of the visible spectrum and at its best in the middle, where the eye can tell the difference between two hues with a wavelength difference of only 1 nm. The figure also shows the discrimination curve for red-blind and green-blind dichromats. This will be referred to in the next chapter on colour vision deficiencies.

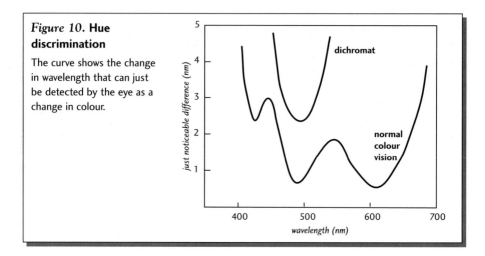

Figure 10. Hue discrimination

The curve shows the change in wavelength that can just be detected by the eye as a change in colour.

The previous chapter introduced the idea of additive colour mixing. By mixing three coloured lights, of the primary colours red, green and blue, almost any colour can be produced. The primary colours used in additive colour mixing are not fixed, but chosen for their practical suitability. They need to be well separated along the spectrum, with the blue blue enough to excite the blue cones and the red red enough to give sufficient differential response between the rather similar red and green cones. That said, the precise wavelengths are not critical. The primary colours shown in Figure 9 are typical of those used in additive mixing experiments. From the curves of spectral sensitivity of the cones, it is straightforward to predict the ratio of primary colours that will be needed to reproduce another coloured light. This calculation has been done and the results show excellent agreement with the results of three-colour mixing experiments. Inspection of Figure 9 helps to explain why it is impossible to match all colours with a mix of three primaries. With some colours the best that can be done is to produce the correct hue, but somewhat unsaturated. This is because the mix of primaries required to match the hue will necessarily stimulate all three sets of cones. This produces a sensation of white light in addition to the sensation of hue and this serves to desaturate the mix.

Colour perception

Elementary science books sometimes show the eye as a camera, with the image on the retina being transmitted to the brain intact - as if there were some sort of inner eye that would then inspect an electrical image within the brain. It is now understood that the brain deals with descriptions of the visual field, rather than an image of it. Further, much

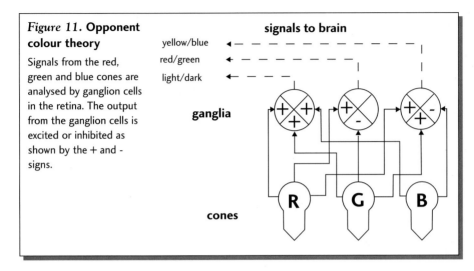

Figure 11. Opponent colour theory

Signals from the red, green and blue cones are analysed by ganglion cells in the retina. The output from the ganglion cells is excited or inhibited as shown by the + and - signs.

signals to brain

yellow/blue

red/green

light/dark

ganglia

cones

of the data processing that converts the retinal image into the signals used by the brain takes place within the retina itself. Between the photoreceptors and the optic nerve, which transmits the signals to the brain, there is a complex network of nerve cells - synapses, bipolar cells and ganglion cells. We will not attempt to give an explanation of their working. They can detect patterns, spatial differences or changes over time in the image on the retina, and produce coded signals to be forwarded to the brain. Their operation can be regarded as a form of data compression. For instance, transmitting the message "nothing has changed" is far more economical than transmitting the same detailed image many times a second. The brain performs even more complex perceptual tasks than the retina and modern research is producing more detailed information as to how these tasks are organised. It has been shown that one area of the brain is dedicated to the recognition of faces, quite separate from the function of recognising other objects. Compared with this, colour perception is almost simple.

While it is clear that some form of colour processing is carried out in the retina, many details are still unresolved. One theory yet to be proved or disproved was put forward by the nineteenth century physiologist Ewald Hering. He proposed that the three colour signals from the cones are combined to provide a dark/light signal, a red/green signal and a blue/yellow signal, as illustrated in **Figure 11**. This model has the attraction of restoring the colour yellow to an important place in the theory of colour vision. Yellow is intuitively perceived as a primary colour and there is a reluctance on the part of many colour theorists to reduce it to the status of a secondary colour. There is some supporting evidence for Hering's model from direct measurement. It is possible to record the response of brain cells in the visual cortex in a monkey while it is looking at different colours. These experiments found some cells that responded to blue/yellow stimuli, and others to green/red. However, Hering's theory is by no means universally accepted.

Colour constancy

When dealing with the sensation of colour in the laboratory, the three-colour theory of colour vision has been outstandingly successful. However, it proves inadequate when dealing with the perception of scenes in real life. The brain constantly interprets what the eye sees in terms of what it "knows" is the actual situation. An example is size constancy. When a person walks away from the observer, the image on the retina gets smaller, but there is no sensation that the person is reducing in actual size. Extend one arm and look at your hand through one eye; bring the other hand so its image overlaps the first, at half an arm's length distance from the eye. The difference in size between the two hand images is surprising, yet normally we are completely unaware of the changing image size when we move our hands. In unfamiliar situations constancy may break down and deliberate manipulation of constancy produces a whole range of optical illusions.

Colour constancy is evidenced by the way familiar coloured objects always look the same colour even under different lighting conditions, say from daylight to artificial light. It is only when direct, side by side comparisons are made of the appearance under different light sources, that we become fully aware that the colour has in fact changed. The colour constancy phenomenon becomes stronger when dealing with the perception of complex real-life scenes. This was extensively investigated by Edwin Land, the inventor of the Polaroid camera. One of his demonstrations involved photographing a still-life of fruit and flowers using only two colours. Separate black and white transparencies were taken of the still-life, using yellow and orange filters. When projected separately, through the appropriate colour filter, the viewer simply saw a monochromatic picture, in shades of either yellow or orange. However when the two were projected simultaneously in register, the image displayed virtually the whole range of colours, reds, greens and blues, which were present in the original scene. These colours were not present in the projected image, yet the perceptual mechanisms in the brain had used cues in the scene to reconstruct what it considered should be there.

It is impossible to produce the sensation of brown or a metallic sheen using a three-colour mixing experiment in the laboratory, where the subject views the colour mixtures as an abstract patch of light. Yet they may be produced by a television set or colour film, which have still only three primary colours to mix. Land developed his own theories of colour perception, where the wavelength of light is not uniquely "colour-making". Rather, the wavelength carries information that assists the brain to *assign* colours to an object, but only in conjunction with clues from other aspects and parts of the image, with a contribution from pre-existing expectations.

Animal vision

The ability to see colour is spread widely throughout the animal kingdom. The investigation of animal colour vision may be categorised into two approaches, physiological and behavioural. It is possible to examine the retina of an animal to discover how many categories of cone exist and measure the ranges of wavelengths that they absorb. However, it is only if the animal can be shown to respond in its behaviour to different colours that it can truly be said to have colour vision. A variety of shrimp has been found to possess 10 different types of colour receptor, sensitive to 10 different colours; however, it is not yet possible to say what this means to the shrimp. Investigating an animal's ability to discriminate colours is not easy and it is a tribute to the skill and patience of the experimenters - not to mention the patience of their subjects - that so much is known. Colour vision implies the ability to distinguish between different colours, based on colour alone and not using other cues such as brightness. We have no problem in following the action in a black and white film, since there is enough information given by the variation in brightness for us to make sense of the scene. It is therefore essential to eliminate the possible effect of brightness, texture and shape when setting up experiments on the colour vision of animals. A typical experiment would be to present the animal with three coloured objects, two of which are the same colour and one of which is slightly different from the others. The animal is trained to select the one that is different; training is normally carried out by offering the animal a reward of food when it selects the correct target. By using monochromatic light as the stimulus, it is possible to build up the wavelength discrimination function for that animal. This is a curve that shows how sensitive the eye is at detecting a small colour difference. To find out more about the colour receptors in an animal's eye it is necessary to do further experiments. Techniques include the presentation of colour mixes, equivalent to the anomaloscope used in assessing colour vision deficiency in humans. In some cases direct measurements of the absorption spectra of the photopigments have been made.

The range of colour vision types found in nature is large. Only blue light can penetrate to the depths of the ocean and deep sea fish tend to be colour-blind, relying solely on rod vision for sensitivity. Tropical fish, living near the surface where bright sunlight penetrates their world, are sensitive to a wide range of colours and have three or four-colour vision. The goldfish is a particularly well studied example of a tetrachromic fish, i.e. one with four types of colour receptor. Freshwater fish, living in waters where mud or algae may restrict the range of coloured illumination available, are often dichromatic. The freshwater rudd even exhibits a seasonal change in the peak wavelength sensitivity of one of its classes of cone. Birds that are active during the day have tetrachromic vision, with an extra (from our point of view) class of receptor that extends sensitivity into the near ultraviolet.

Insects have a completely different type of eye from the familiar lens and retina system found in humans and other mammals. The compound eye of a bee consists of thousands of facets, each with its own lens that refracts light onto a photosensitive structure consisting of several types of receptor cell. No image of the view is formed, as happens on the mammalian retina. Rather, each facet sends a signal to the brain, containing information on brightness and colour. Since each facet is hard wired to the brain, the brain can tell which direction the incident light came from and can reconstruct a map of the field of view. Vision in the bee has been well studied, largely because the bee is amenable to training and will patiently continue to search for food among a set of variously coloured artificial flowers provided by the experimenter. The bee has trichromatic colour vision, which extends further into the ultraviolet than does human vision. Photographs of flowers taken in ultra violet light often show increased contrast between the centre of the flower and the surrounding petals, compared with the human view. This may well assist the bee to home in on its target when collecting nectar. A species of desert ant has been found with four types of photoreceptor and a butterfly with five. So far the butterfly has proved resistant to training and the implications for its colour vision are still unclear.

Nearly all mammals have two-colour vision and so are able to see colours in more or less the same way as a red-blind or green-blind human; these terms will be defined fully in the next chapter. However, some mammals operate in a world where there is little light and being able to see colour is of little advantage. Here, perhaps, evolution has operated in reverse and several mammals are colour-blind. Some nocturnal rodents, including the rat, are monochromats and have a single class of cone receptors operating in the green part of the spectrum. The same is true for most marine mammals that live in the sea, where the illumination is predominantly bluish. Cats and dogs are dichromats, though in the case of the cats this has had to be inferred from electrophysiological measurements. Cats in the laboratory have shown no interest in responding to coloured stimuli and it has been impossible to train them.

As far as is known, apes and monkeys of the Old World are the only mammals with the same trichromatic colour vision as man. New World primates, i.e. those living in North and South America, have dichromatic colour vision and would be classified as protanopes in human terms. However, recent research has shown the position to be more complicated. The squirrel monkeys are the most common primates in riverside forests of Central America, the Guianas, and the Amazon River basin. All males and some females are dichromats, while other females are trichromats. The single red-green pigment in the dichromats and the two red-green pigments found in the trichromats may be any combination from three possible red-green pigments. In other words, there are three different genes for the red-green photopigment. A male squirrel monkey can receive only one of them, a female may receive any two; if she gets the same gene from both parents, she will be dichromatic.

Evolution

Rudimentary vision is found even in single cell animals; the pond dwelling *Euglena viridis* can distinguish between light of different intensities, enabling it to swim towards light, but avoid direct sunlight. From primitive light-sensitive creatures such as this, the image forming eye evolved step by step over a long period of time. It has been argued that the advent of the eye was a major force in triggering the Cambrian explosion, that time 500 million years ago when the world saw a rapid increase in the rate of evolution and the introduction of a multiplicity of novel life forms. Once some animals could see to hunt, natural selection was driven by the relation between predators and prey. There is evidence that creatures in the Cambrian sea were highly coloured, producing iridescent colours by means of fine diffraction gratings; this carries the implication that colour vision was also developed. By observing the wide range of primitive eyes present in both living animals and fossils, it is possible to piece together a plausible route by which our eyes have developed. This has been described in many books on evolution. We will concentrate on the arrival of colour vision and take for granted the evolution of the image forming eye, complete with lens and retina.

The most important function of the eye is the detection of shape and movement. This can be done adequately with an eye containing only a single type of receptor, giving monochromatic vision. The owner of the eye has the same amount of information available as in a black and white film - which is a lot, and adequate for many purposes. However, the ability to discriminate colours confers an advantage and developed a long time ago, before mammals evolved. It is likely that the first primitive eyes had a single class of cones only. This gave sharp monochromatic vision. The cones had maximum sensitivity in the middle of the spectrum where the sun's light is at its most energetic, and thus corresponded to the green cones of the present human eye. A long time ago, probably before mammals had evolved, a second class of cone was added that was sensitive to blue light, giving dichromatic colour vision, qualitatively similar to a colour-blind human. The function of the short wave cones is to provided colour information. Most of the basic functions of vision, such as recognition of shape, discrimination of detail and detection of pattern and movement, are carried out by the middle wave cones. It is sufficient for colour discrimination to provide extra colour information from a relatively small number of short wave cones, spread over the fovea and mingled with the other cones.

Dichromatic colour vision, with the middle wave cones providing the detail and a few blue cones to give colour perception, is common to most mammals. Following Professor Mollon of Cambridge University, we term this the ancient system. At some stage in the last 30 million years, the middle wave receptors split to give the red and green receptors that today are found in man and many Old World primates. Present thinking in evolution rejects the idea that organisms evolve and 'get better' or 'improve'. Rather, organisms evolve in response to a changed environment; there is no better or worse, just appropriateness to the environment of the time. The contemporary environment that an organism exists within is not static, but contains other animals and plants that are themselves evolving. It may be that different organisms co-evolve, responding to and reinforcing the evolutionary changes in each other. This seems to be what happened in the development of three-colour vision in Old World primates. About 30 million years ago, some tropical trees began developing fruits that provided ideal food for monkeys and apes. The fruits were large enough to be worth eating by a monkey and too large to be taken by a bird. This meant that the tree could no longer rely on birds to disperse the seeds contained in the fruits and so required an alternative means of ensuring that the seeds were dispersed widely. The fruits were coloured yellow or orange when ripe and this is a difficult colour for a dichromat to spot against a background of green leaves. The characteristics used when searching a visual field for an object are shape, brightness contrast and colour contrast. The dappled background of a leafy tree, with many variations in both shape and in light and shade make the first two characteristics of little value in the search for fruit. This effect is utilised in the Ishihara colour deficiency tests, where the confused background of coloured dots ensures that the subject is forced to rely on colour contrast to read the hidden figure. The colour deficient person is unable to utilise cues based on brightness, texture or shape. A dichromatic monkey, or a red-green colour-blind person, is at a great disadvantage in searching for ripe fruit in a tree. Indeed, this was one of the earliest recorded observations on the problems faced by colour-blind people. An early nineteenth century description of a protanope, who surprisingly had taken up a career as a fruit farmer:

> "He cannot discern, even in a loaded bush, the existence of red gooseberries among the leaves, until he has almost approached so near as to be able to take hold of the branch. Rosy apples on a tree, which my be discovered by ordinary eyes at a distance of from thirty to forty yards at least, are lost to his sense, until he has come within ten or twenty yards of the tree, when he can trace out the fruit by its form."

The problem is illustrated in **Figure 12** (see page 67), which uses a computer transformation to show how leaves and fruit appear to a colour-blind person.

It was therefore to the mutual advantage of tree and monkey for the tree to develop large edible fruits and for the monkey to develop a new form of colour vision that would allow it to readily locate the ripe fruit against a background of leaves. The monkey gains a source of food and the tree ensures wide dispersal of the seed contained in the fruit, as the monkey defecates or spits them out. This scenario is supported by genetic evidence. The gene for the blue receptor is carried on chromosome 7 and has little in common with the red and green wavelength genes. The genes responsible for coding the red and green photopigments are located close to each other on the X chromosome. Recent work in molecular genetics has shown that the red and green genes have some 96% of their code sequence in common. The implication is that this is a relatively recent evolutionary development and that the two genes have not yet settled down with distinct identities.

Summary: Colour vision

Light is detected by photoreceptors in the retina of the eye. There are two types of photoreceptor, rods and cones, named after their shape. Rods are responsible for night vision. They are very sensitive to low light levels, but are dazzled by bright light. Rods have no colour sense. Cones are responsible for normal acute colour vision in daylight. There are three types of cone, termed red, green and blue, which are sensitive to the long, middle and short wavelength regions of the spectrum. Coloured light falling on the retina produces responses in the three types of cone according to the distribution of wavelengths in the light. These responses are analysed by the brain to produce a sensation of colour. The perception of a coloured object is modified by the brain's expectation of how it should look. This is termed colour constancy and may give rise to colour illusions in some circumstances.

Many animals possess colour vision. A variety of types of vision have evolved in response to environmental stimuli. Many birds have four-colour vision, as does the goldfish. Nearly all mammals have two-colour vision, corresponding to the green and blue cones in the human eye. Man and apes and monkeys of the Old World are the only mammals with three-colour vision. It is supposed that trichromatic vision evolved to provide a benefit when searching for ripe fruit among green leaves.

Chapter 3 - Colour vision deficiencies

The importance of colour vision to early man was above all in enabling him to locate food and to judge the quality of fruit and vegetation. Since most of the population lived on the land until the industrial revolution, it is surprising that the common problem of colour blindness in men seems to have gone unnoticed until relatively recently. A scientific paper of 1777 records the first clear description of inherited colour blindness. Two brothers had difficulty in naming colours and had problems in locating fruit on the tree, having to find cherries among the leaves by their size and shape. It was noted at the time that the brothers were intelligent, perhaps implying that those people who made errors in colour naming were considered somewhat dim.

John Dalton

The first serious study of colour vision deficiency was made by John Dalton in 1794. Dalton is best known for his pioneering work on the atomic theory of matter. As with many scientists of that time, his range of interests was wide and as a young man he pursued studies in botany. He was a Quaker, and as such Dalton was barred from the major universities; in 1793 he was appointed a teacher of mathematics in New College Manchester. One year later he read his paper *Extraordinary facts relating to the vision of colours with observations*. In a letter to his cousin he wrote:

> *"I am at present engaged in a very curious investigation: I discovered last summer with certainty, that colours appear different to me what they do to others: The flowers of most of the Cranesbills appear to me in the day, almost exactly sky blue, whilst others call them deep pink."*

He goes on to describe a visit to a dyers, where he discussed colours of various cloths and was unable to distinguish between some green and red cloths. In a statement that will ring true to many colour-blind people today, he observed *"In short, my observations have afforded a fund of diversion to all."*

Dalton set about investigating his condition, which was shared by his brother. He sought out fellow sufferers and showed that the condition ran in families. Dalton himself thought that his condition was caused by a blue coloration of the jelly-like humour that fills the eyeball. He supposed this to absorb red light and so reduce the sensitivity of the eye to the red end of the spectrum. Dalton persisted in this view until his death in 1844. However Thomas Young had come up with the right idea as early as 1807, when he suggested that there might be "*an absence or paralysis of those fibres of the retina which are calculated to perceive red*". Dalton instructed that a post mortem be carried out on his eyes; the humour was found to be colourless. From his own descriptions of his colour vision problems, it had long been supposed that Dalton was red-blind. However, sufficient tissue from Dalton's eye had been preserved at Manchester to allow a genetic analysis to be performed 150 years later, when he was identified as having been green-blind. Although Dalton failed to identify the cause of his colour blindness, he is universally acknowledged as the man who laid the foundation for the investigation of abnormal colour vision. The condition is still widely referred to as Daltonism, though perhaps more commonly in Europe than in Britain. A colour-blind person in France is referred to as *un daltonien*, or less frequently as *une daltonienne*.

Nomenclature

The preferred term for colour blindness is colour vision deficiency. This emphasises that those with the condition are not "colour-blind" as such, but deficient in the way that they see colours. The various types and degrees of colour vision deficiency have acquired a rather forbidding scientific nomenclature. The terms used by professionals to classify the deficiencies are not self-explanatory; this book will use some simpler terms.

Colour vision deficiency is the preferred term to describe all types of colour deficiency, from a mild defect to the complete absence of colour vision. However, **colour-blind**, while strictly inaccurate, is the common English term used to describe all types of colour vision deficiency. This is largely a matter of linguistic convenience: it is easier to say "he is colour-blind" than "he suffers from colour vision deficiency". To avoid any possible negative connotation arising from the words "blind" or "deficient", the term **Daltonism** is often proposed. This is in common use in Europe and in academic circles, but has yet to be adopted in common speech.

The standard classification of colour vision deficiencies is as follows.

Dichromatism. One of the three colour receptor mechanisms is missing, probably resulting from a lack of the relevant cone pigment. There are therefore three types of dichromatism:

- **protanopia.** The eye lacks the long wavelength or red pigment. There is an inability to see dark reds and there is typically confusion between reds, greens and browns, and between various shades of purple.

- **deuteranopia**. The eye lacks the middle wavelength or green pigment. All colours are seen and there is typically confusion between reds and greens, and blues and purples.

- **tritanopia**. This is a rare condition with impaired sensitivity to blue. There is typically confusion between the colours blue and green.

Anomalous trichromatism. Colour vision deficiency is more commonly caused by altered sensitivity in one of the three receptor mechanisms, rather than by the complete absence of one of them. The wavelength at which maximum sensitivity occurs is shifted from the normal position. The severity of the defect ranges from extreme, where the person is almost a dichromat, to very mild. There are three forms of anomalous trichromatism, depending upon which mechanism has altered sensitivity.

- **protanomaly**. The sensitivity of the red receptor mechanism is displaced from the normal position.

- **deuteranomaly**. This is the most common form of colour vision deficiency. The peak sensitivity of the middle wave receptor is displaced.

- **tritanomaly**. A rare condition, with altered sensitivity of the blue receptor mechanism.

Achromatopsia is also known as **monochromatism** and is characterised by a total inability to distinguish colours. **Typical achromatopsia**, also known as **rod monochromatism**, is caused by an absence of cone receptors in the retina. All vision is by means of the rod receptors and in effect the person only has night vision. There is also a very rare defect known as **atypical achromatopsia** or **cone monochromatism,** where colour vision is absent but the cones appear normal; probably the problem lies somewhere in the brain rather than in the eye itself.

The nomenclature dates back to the early 19th Century and was formalised by the great German physicist Helmholtz. The rather curious choice of words was based on protanopia being the "first" form of colour vision deficiency, deuteranopia the "second" and so on. The terms are modified when used as an adjective or to describe the person with the deficiency, according to the following table.

Table 6. The nomenclature of colour vision deficiency

The condition	The person	The adjective	Symbol
Dichromatism, dichromacy	Dichromat	Dichromatic	
protanopia	protanope	protanopic	P
deuteranopia	deuteranope	deuteranopic	D
tritanopia	tritanope	tritanopic	T
Anomalous trichromatism	Anomalous trichromat		
protanomaly	protonomal	protanomalous	PA
deuteranomaly	deuteranomal	deuteranomalous	DA
tritanomaly	tritanomal	tritanomalous	TA
Achromatopsia	Achromat	Achromatic	

The collective terms protan, deutan and tritan are used to include both the dichromatic and anomalous type of deficiency. Thus the term protan includes both protanopia and protanomaly. The above classification covers all the inherited colour vision deficiencies. It is also possible to acquire defects by disease or exposure to toxic materials. These problems will be discussed below.

The above terms are accepted internationally among scientists, but have not passed into common use. The relative obscurity of the technical terms has inhibited their use and consequently hindered understanding of the important differences between the various types of colour vision deficiency. Accordingly, this book will adopt terms that are simple, precise and descriptive: see **Table 7**.

Table 7. Simplified terminology

Formal Term	New Term
protanopic	red-blind
deuteranopic	green-blind
tritanopic	blue-blind
protanomalous	red-weak
deuteranomalous	green-weak
tritanomalous	blue-weak
achromatic	achromatic

The green-weak deficiency is the most common form of colour blindness found in the general population. The approximate distribution is shown in **Table 8**.

Table 8. **Occurrence of colour vision deficiencies in the UK**

Condition		Proportion (%)	
		Male	**Female**
Protanopia	Red-blind	1.0	0.01
Deuteranopia	Green-blind	1.0	0.01
Tritanopia	Blue blind	very small	very small
Protanomaly	Red-weak	1.0	0.03
Deuteranomaly	Green-weak	5.0	0.35
Tritanomaly	Blue-weak	very small	very small

The distribution of colour vision deficiency is not uniform over the world. In general, the incidence is high in urban, industrialised regions and is low among nomadic or hunting populations. *Figure 13* (see page 68) gives an idea of the global distribution for deficiency in males. The incidence in males ranges from 8% in Europe, North America and Australia, to 2% among Inuit peoples and desert nomads. In looking at this, it must be remembered that the cause of the deficiency is genetic, so the cause of the variation must be looked for in ancestry rather than geography. The incidence of colour vision deficiency in North America is determined by the predominantly European background of the population, rather than by any environmental conditions in the New World.

Evolutionary explanations have been advanced. Colour vision deficiency would be a severe handicap for a hunter-gatherer and natural selection would be expected to keep the incidence low in such societies. This would no longer apply once societies became settled and the division of labour developed. There seems to be a correlation between the proportion of colour vision defectives in a population and the time that has elapsed since the hunting stage. There can be variations over quite a small area. Eastern Scotland has an incidence of 5%, while south west England achieves 9% of males with colour vision deficiencies. Inbreeding can distort figures for isolated communities. This was memorably described by Oliver Sacks in his book *Island of the Colour Blind*, where he visited an island in the Pacific that had a remarkably high incidence of achromatopsia.

Chromaticity diagram

In Chapter 2 we briefly mentioned the phenomenon of additive colour mixing, where a mixture of two or more coloured lights is seen by the eye as a single, but different, colour. The way in which the eye combines the different colours into a single resulting colour is fundamental to an understanding of colour vision, and by extension to an understanding of colour vision deficiency. The most effective way of showing how the eye combines colours is by using the **CIE chromaticity diagram**. This diagram has been used for years as a fundamental tool by experts in the fields of colour technology and lighting design, but is relatively little known outside these professions. At first sight, the diagram looks unfamiliar, but the small amount of effort required to understand it is well worthwhile. It provides the most effective way of understanding the colour confusions experienced by different classes of colour defective people. We have already seen how the attributes of a colour can be expressed as a combination of its hue, saturation and lightness; the Munsell system displays these three dimensions in a 3-D solid. For many purposes connected with colour it is sufficient to consider hue and saturation alone, which together make up the **chromaticity** of a colour. By dealing with only two dimensions, the relationship between different colours can be represented on a flat two dimensional diagram, which is much easier to handle and understand. The missing dimension is lightness.

The chromaticity diagram was standardised by the CIE (Commission Internationale de l'Eclairage) in 1931 and is shown in *Figure 14* (see page 68). Since the diagram deals with the way colours look to the human eye, it was necessary for the CIE to define a standard human observer, i.e. a person with the most normal colour vision imaginable. The chromaticity diagram therefore works for this ideal viewer; some slight differences are to be expected among real people, even those with normal colour vision. A colour is positioned on the diagram by a pair of co-ordinates x and y, where x and y represent proportions of theoretical "supersaturated" red and green primaries. The proportion of the blue primary is given by $z = 1 - (x+y)$, i.e. the sum total of the three primaries remains constant at unity. The supersaturated primaries are mathematical conveniences and need not worry us any more. Look again at the diagram. All pure spectral colours can be plotted along the horseshoe shaped curve running from red light at 700 nm wavelength to blue at 400 nm. The family of purples falls along the straight line joining the extremes of red and blue. All visible colours lie within the envelope. As we move inwards from the envelope, the colours become more unsaturated, until white light is reached at the point W in the middle. Needless to say, it required an international committee to define exactly what is meant by white light. Think of it as light that contains equal proportions of all visible wavelengths.

A most useful property of the chromaticity diagram is that it shows directly the results of mixing two colours together. The additive mixture of two colours always lies on the straight line joining them on the diagram. The position of the resultant mixture along the line depends on the proportions of the two original colours in the mix. More precisely, the distance from the resultant mixture to each constituent is inversely proportional to the proportion of that constituent in the mixture. It follows that any spectral colour is joined to its complementary colour by a line passing through the achromatic point W; remember that the definition of a complementary colour is that a colour and its complementary can be mixed to produce white light.

Any colour has a dominant wavelength associated with it, which is plotted on the chromaticity diagram by drawing a line from the white point W (known technically as the achromatic point), through the point representing the colour and extending it to meet the boundary. This shows that any colour may be considered as a mixture of its dominant

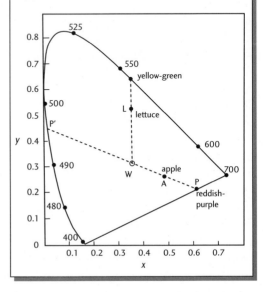

Figure 15. Dominant wavelengths

The lettuce leaf at L is a yellow-green colour, with dominant wavelength 560 nm.

The reddish apple at A has a colour with complementary wavelength 495 nm.

wavelength plus white. Where the dominant colour lies on the non-spectral purple region of the boundary, it cannot of course be defined as a spectral wavelength. The point A represents a red apple, which appears as a purplish red. The line from the achromatic point intersects the boundary at the saturated purple-red at P. The dominant colour is then defined in terms of the complementary of P, which in this case has a wavelength of 495 nm. The dominant colour or hue of the apple is described as "complementary dominant wavelength 495 nm".

There is no unique set of primary colours to be used for additive mixing. In practice, the three colours are chosen to be widely separated. The more widely separated they are, the greater gamut of colours that can be produced. **Figure 16** shows the primary colours produced by the phosphors in a colour television set. Any colour that lies inside the area of the triangle can be reproduced by mixing the three primaries. Colours that lie outside the triangle cannot be accurately reproduced on the screen. In practice, this is not a great problem. It was mentioned in the last chapter how effective the brain is at providing its own contribution to the perception of a coloured scene. It is impossible to choose three primaries that will produce all possible colours seen by the eye. Looking at the chromaticity curve, the curved left hand edge will always lie outside any straight edged triangle. Pure blue-greens cannot be reproduced accurately, but will always be somewhat desaturated.

Dichromacy

Dichromats lack one of the three cone photopigments in the retina. This has been shown directly by experiment in the case of red-blind

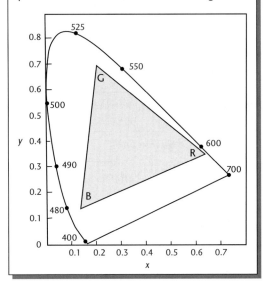

Figure 16. Additive colour mixing

Mixing the RGB colours in a television tube can produce all colours within the shaded triangle.

and green-blind people. The lack of blue photopigment in blue-blind people may be assumed, though it has not been possible to demonstrate experimentally. The lack of one out of the three colour mechanisms of course has serious effects on the ability to see and distinguish colours. The effect on colour sensation is hard to convey. Remember that the dichromat sees the world as "normally" coloured to them and it is only when comparing notes with a normal trichromat that problems are revealed. For the moment, we will consider the consequences of dichromacy that can be measured objectively. These mostly concern the ability to match, mix or distinguish between colours.

We have seen how most, but not all, colours can be reproduced by a mixture of three primary colours. The dichromat requires only two colours to perform a colour match for the full range of hues. The chromaticity diagram is a powerful way of illustrating the consequences of dichromacy in diagrammatic form. Although the diagram may look a bit forbidding at first sight, it repays a little study. Once understood, the diagram illustrates both clearly and simply the likely colour confusions and difficulties experienced by a dichromat. For each type of dichromat it is possible to draw a family of straight lines on the chromaticity diagram, such that all colours represented by points along one of the lines may look the same to a dichromat viewer. Colours along the line have the same hue and saturation to a dichromat and will look identical if the lightness is adjusted. The lines are termed **confusion lines** or **isochromatic lines**. More strictly, they are sometimes termed **pseudo-isochromatic** lines to emphasise that they only appear to be the same colour to a dichromat.

Figure 17 shows a set of confusion lines for a red-blind person. This shows immediately that there is little discrimination between colours with wavelengths ranging all the way from 525 (green) to 700 nm (red). The practical consequence is that a red-blind person can match a yellow spectral light with virtually any combination of red and green. Remember that the diagram does not show brightness; the red-blind person sees red as

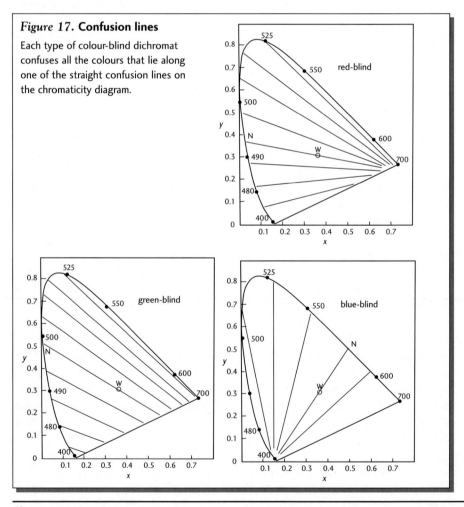

Figure 17. Confusion lines

Each type of colour-blind dichromat confuses all the colours that lie along one of the straight confusion lines on the chromaticity diagram.

very dark, so adjustments have to be made to the intensity of the red light to compensate in a mixing test. The red-blind person can therefore be expected to have poor discrimination between colours positioned along the top right hand edge of the curve running from red to green. Discrimination improves once the curve goes round the corner and goes from green to blue. The range of non-spectral purples along the bottom will also be poorly discriminated.

One of the confusion lines in the diagram passes through the white point W. Thus the red-blind observer will confuse all colours along this line, running from blue-green to reddish purple, and including grey in the middle. In this example the lightness of the white at point W would have to be reduced to grey to provide a match with other colours along the line. This confusion line meets the envelope at the **neutral point**, shown as N in the figure, which is a blue-green hue with a wavelength of 494 nm. It is perhaps an unexpected fact that there is a unique hue, plus its complement, that cannot be distinguished from grey by a red-blind person. Corresponding diagrams for green-blind and blue-blind dichromats are shown. In each case the set of confusion lines converge to a point, though the exact position of the point may differ among individuals.

Comparison of the diagrams for red-blind and green-blind dichromats shows that they suffer rather similar problems. Both types cannot distinguish between spectral colours with a wavelength above 525 nm, i.e. all colours between green and red. The neutral points lie at similar wavelengths to each other: 494 for red-blind and 498 nm for green-blind. This small difference is measurable experimentally, but the variation between individual dichromats is sufficiently large for the neutral point to be an unreliable method for differentiating between red and green-blind dichromats. The greatest difference between the red-blind and green-blind confusion lines occurs along the lower, non-spectral boundary of the curve. Green-blind dichromats can be expected to be much better than red-blind in making distinctions among the family of purples. This effect is exploited in diagnostic tests that are used to distinguish between the two types of dichromat.

The blue-blind diagram is quite different from the other two. The range of colours from green to red is clearly seen and no difficulties are to be expected when using the anomaloscope. The problems arise down the left hand boundary of the curve, where colours between 510 and 400 nm will be difficult to distinguish from one another, i.e. the colour range from green to blue. The neutral point lies in the yellow with a wavelength of 572 nm.

When the confusion lines were established by experiment in the 1930s, steps of just noticeable difference in wavelength were measured. Red-blind subjects could differentiate among 17 wavelengths, and green-blind among 27. This has to be compared with the 150 wavelengths distinguished by the normal trichromat. It may be pointed out here that several researchers consider that dichromats should be thought of as seeing only two hues, blue and yellow. Dichromats tend to interpret changes in saturation or brightness as a change in hue. The result is that they think they can see more colours than they actually can.

Anomalous trichromatism

Dichromatism, the complete absence of one of the photopigments, gives a colour deficiency that is explicable on the chromaticity diagram and consistent in its characteristics. Red-blind people have the same difficulties as each other and green-blind the same as other green-blind (more or less: there are minor variations). However, as was shown in Table 8, the majority of colour deficient people are classed as **anomalous trichromats**. They have three separate sets of photoreceptors, but the wavelength response of one of them is shifted from normal. The condition of anomalous trichromatism is effectively described in terms of the so-called **Rayleigh match.**

Normal trichromats can match a monochromatic yellow light with a mixture of red and green lights. This phenomenon was investigated by Lord Rayleigh towards the end of the nineteenth century. Colour theory seems to have attracted more than its share of great men and Rayleigh was one of them. He did pioneering work in acoustics, explained why the sky is blue and got the Nobel prize for his part in the discovery of the rare gas argon. Rayleigh measured the quantities of red and green light required to match yellow and recorded the results for many people. Most produced about the same mixture, but some needed excessive quantities of either red or green light to achieve a match. Dichromats can produce a match with any given combination of red and green, adjusting only the brightness of the yellow light. Rayleigh's observations produced the first record of anomalous trichromatism, that is, three-colour vision, but different from normal. The method of mixing red and green has come to be known as a Rayleigh match and is the basis of the anomaloscope used in the diagnosis of defective colour vision.

In a red-weak person, the green photoreceptors are normal, but the red receptors have their spectral absorption curve shifted towards green; an example is shown in *Figure 18*. The corresponding situation holds for the green-weak. The term adopted here of weak does not imply that there are fewer receptors or that they are less sensitive. It is the shift in spectral response that produces the anomalous colour vision. Anomalous trichromatism covers the whole range from **extreme anomaly**, i.e. almost a dichromat, to a weak form where colour vision is almost normal. For people with normal colour vision, the separation between the peak sensitive wavelengths for the red and green receptors is 30 nm. For those with the weak form of colour vision deficiency, the separation between the two peaks may be anything from 1 nm to nearly 30 nm. Clearly, this separation will determine how good or bad is their colour vision, and this has been shown experimentally in the laboratory. Conventional screening tests for colour blindness, such as the Ishihara, do not discriminate between those with a severe or with a very mild form of colour vision deficiency. This leads to some people with almost normal vision being excluded from jobs that they are capable of performing perfectly well.

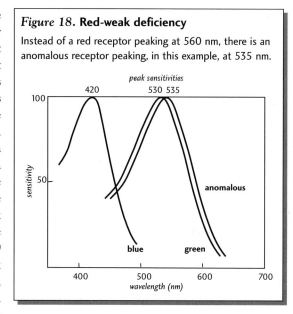

Figure 18. **Red-weak deficiency**

Instead of a red receptor peaking at 560 nm, there is an anomalous receptor peaking, in this example, at 535 nm.

Small field tritanopia

It was pointed out in the last chapter that blue cones account for only a small proportion, about 3%, of the cones in the central part of the retina. At the very centre of the fovea there is an area about 100 μm across where there are no blue cones at all. If the eye is concentrating on a very small coloured object, there is a chance that the image on the retina may not fall on even a single blue cone. If this happens, the eye is effectively blue-blind. This effect occurs when the angle subtended by the object at the eye is less than 0.5°. This is about the angular size of a tennis ball seen from a distance equal to the width of a singles tennis court.

The phenomenon is known as small field tritanopia, or sometimes as foveal tritanopia where the central region without blue cones is implicated. Although all colour normals, and colour defectives as well, experience this effect, few are aware of it. It has some practical consequences. Small field tritanopia makes it difficult to distinguish pale yellow objects from white objects of a similar size when seen against a blue background. This proved a problem when searching for aircraft rescue dinghies in a stormy sea and their colour was altered from yellow to orange to make detection easier.

Large field trichromacy

The previous paragraph showed that a colour normal becomes defective when viewing very small images. It seems that the reverse applies when a colour-blind person views large areas of colour. The explanation of colour deficiency in this chapter shows clearly that red-blind and green-blind dichromats are unable to distinguish between red and green; this is borne out by tests using the anomaloscope. However, many, if not all, dichromats would claim to experience a definite sensation of red when looking at a large, bright, red object; this experience is quite distinct from the sensation of green. The explanation lies in the size of the image on the retina. Most experiments on colour vision ask the subject to view a coloured target, whether an object or spot of light, which subtends an angle at the eye of about 2 degrees. This means that the image of the target on the retina approximately covers the fovea, i.e. the region that is densely populated with cones. This size corresponds to looking at a target of diameter 10mm from a distance of 300mm.

With this size of target, there is no doubt that red and green-blind dichromats are indeed red-green colour blind. They will accept any mixture of red and green when tested using an anomaloscope, as shown in Figure 27. However, if the size of the coloured light is increased, dichromats improve their performance and behave as if they had the weak form of colour deficiency. In other words, they can now distinguish between red and green. What seems to be happening is that the large image on the retina now falls onto the area outside the fovea and so falls on the rod type of photoreceptor. The brain now gets three colour signals, two from the dichromat's two types of cone, and the other from the rods. The subject now operates with a form of trichromacy and can make colour distinctions that were impossible with a small target. The relevant experiments were done with a target size of 8 degrees, four times the size of the standard foveal target.

At times, red-blind people have been greeted with scepticism when they claim to experience something as "bright red". From the explanation above, it seems that they can. What relation their red sensation has to that of a colour normal is open to conjecture.

Genetic inheritance

The common forms of red-green colour vision deficiency are inherited. The genes responsible for the defects are classified as sex-linked recessive. The practical consequence of this is that transmission of the characteristic is via the mother, and that colour vision deficiency is suffered mostly by her sons. The inheritance of colour vision deficiency is a clear example of classical genetics as first described by Mendel in the 19th century. Colour vision deficiency is caused by variation in a single gene, which is either normal or variant. This makes for a very straightforward pattern of inheritance, compared with an attribute such as height, which is influenced by the combined effect of many genes. Recent advances in experimental genetics have explored the detailed structure of the genes responsible for colour vision deficiency and have succeeded in showing how the weak (anomalous) forms of deficiency are caused. For the moment, we will lump dichromacy and anomalous trichromacy together and discuss the inheritance of red and green colour blindness. The recent discoveries will be described later.

The genetic blueprint that determines the characteristics of an individual is held on 23 chromosome pairs, which reside in the cell nucleus. The fertilised cell at conception contains a complete set of chromosomes and all the information that will determine the eventual characteristics of that person. We can side-step the entire nature-nurture debate about the relative influence of genes and the environment on the subsequent development of an individual person. Red-green colour vision deficiency is entirely genetic in causation and unaffected by anything else.

We will make no attempt here to go into the structure of DNA or the means by which genetic information is encoded. It is sufficient to know that the genes that code for the red and green pigments are located on the 23rd chromosome pair. However, the 23rd chromosome pair is special, in that it differs between males and females. The female pair contains two X chromosomes and the male pair contains one X and one Y chromosome. At conception, a female inherits one X chromosome from her mother and the other X from her father. The male inherits the X from his mother and the Y from his father.

The X chromosome carries a large number of genes, each of which carries a particular piece of information and always occupies the same situation or **locus** on the chromosome. Chapter 3 discussed how the cones in the retina carry 3 types of photopigment for the red, green and blue regions of the spectrum. The gene for the blue photopigment is carried on the 7th chromosome pair and the mechanism for inheritance is quite different from that being described in this section. The genes that encode for the production of the red and green photopigments are carried on loci that are situated near to each other on the X chromosome. Either gene may be defective. A range of defects is possible, resulting in either a total lack of the photopigment, giving rise to dichromacy, or a displaced colour response, giving rise to anomalous trichromacy. In this discussion, the different types of red-green colour vision defect are considered together; only one type of defect can be expressed at one time. The inheritance pattern is the same for all red and green defects. In this discussion, we refer to the normal red and green genes as R and G, and the defective versions as R* and G*. *Figure 19* shows a schematic diagram of the male and female chromosomes showing the locus of the red and green genes. The female chromosome pair contains two versions of each gene and the male chromosome pair only one. It is this fact that accounts for the difference in incidence of colour vision deficiency between men and women.

Figure 19. **Genes for colour deficiency**

In the carrier female, the normal gene G is dominant over the recessive deficient gene G*. A male with a deficient G* gene suffers from green-weak colour deficiency.

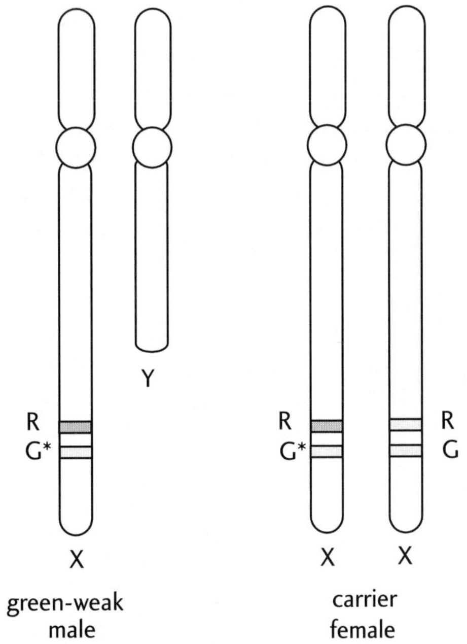

The deficiency genes R* and G* are said to be **recessive**, while the normal R and G genes are **dominant**. A female carrying a single deficiency gene has normal colour vision, since the normal gene at the same locus on the other X chromosome dominates over the recessive version and determines the outcome. Since the Y chromosome plays no part in colour vision, a deficient gene on the single male X chromosome is enough to cause colour blindness.

The possible combinations are set out in **Table 9**, together with the proportions of the population with each combination of genes. The proportions are typical of those found in a European population. The male distribution is known directly from surveys of colour vision; the female proportions have been calculated using the laws of genetics and agree with the observed frequencies set out in Table 8. The female chromosome can carry six different combinations of the red and green genes. For a woman to be colour-blind, it is necessary that both branches of the chromosome carry a deficient gene at the same locus; this is the consequence of a recessive gene. It may be surprising to note that it is possible for a woman to carry both the R* and G* genes at the same time. All her sons will be colour-blind, with a 50/50 chance of being either red or green deficient. She would not be expected to have defective colour vision herself, since each gene is dominated by the normal version on the other branch of the chromosome. There is, however, evidence that some such females may show red-weak defects. Comparison of the incidence for males and females shows that while 8% of the male population carry a colour deficiency gene, a total of 16% of women do so. This can be seen intuitively. Since the son of a woman carrying a deficient has a 50% chance of being colour-blind, the proportion of female carriers must be twice the proportion of colour-blind males.

Table 9. **Possible gene distributions on 23rd chromosome**

X	Y	Males (observed)		Proportion (%)
R G		normal		92
R* G		red deficient		2
R G*		green deficient		6

X	X	Females (calculated)		
RG	RG	normal vision	non-carrier	84.66
RG	R*G	normal vision	red deficiency carrier	3.70
RG	RG*	normal vision	green deficiency carrier	11.00
R* G	R* G	red deficient	red deficiency carrier	0.04
R G*	R G*	green deficient	green deficiency carrier	0.36
R* G	R G*	normal vision	red and green deficiency carrier	0.24

The possible combinations of parental genes and the outcome on the colour vision of daughters is shown in more detail in **Table 10**. The expected frequency of each type of defect in the table is found by multiplying the parental frequencies, then dividing by 2, since there is an equal chance of the daughter inheriting a normal or defective X chromosome from the mother. The sum total for each type of deficiency is shown in the final column. Daughters who inherit a PA gene from one parent and a D or DA from the other parent may sometimes have a red-weak deficiency. The situation is not clear and is indicated by a question mark in the table.

Table 10. Distribution of colour vision deficiency in females

The frequency of different genes in father and mother is shown in the first row and column. The intersection shows the type of deficiency in a daughter and the expected frequency in the population.

Carrier mother (X)	Father (X)				Daughters
	P (1%)	PA (1%)	D (1%)	DA (5%)	
P (2%)	P (0.01%)	PA (0.01%)			P (0.01%)
PA (2%)	PA (0.01%)	PA (0.01%)	?	?	PA (0.03%)
D (2%)		?	D (0.01%)	DA (0.05%)	D (0.01%)
DA(10%)		?	DA (0.05%)	DA (0.25%)	DA (0.35%)

Most of the possible patterns of inherited colour vision deficiency are shown in the diagrams. **Figure 20** (see page 70) shows the outcomes of various relationships where everyone involved is either normal or suffers from a red deficiency defect; the pattern is exactly the same for green deficiency. The diagram shows, in example VI, that colour deficiency in a male may skip a generation. A colour defective male most commonly has a colour defective grandfather; in some cases it may be a colour defective mother (IV) or defective great grandfather (VI). **Figure 21** (see page 71) illustrates some situations where both red and green deficiencies are present in the family. This introduces the character of the dual carrier female. She carries two types of defective gene, a red deficiency gene on one X chromosome and a green deficiency gene on the other. All her sons will be colour-blind, and some boys may exhibit a different colour deficiency from their brothers (IV).

The straightforward description above does not differentiate between dichromacy and anomalous trichromacy, e.g. between red-blind and red-weak deficiencies. The genes for the two forms of deficiency are carried at the same locus on the chromosome, so that they are inherited in the same way as each other. It is possible for the two genes to appear at the same locus on opposite halves of a female chromosome, e.g. with the red-weak gene on one half and the red-blind on the other. When this happens, the mild defect is dominant over the severe form, so she will exhibit a red-weak colour deficiency. Half her sons will be dichromats (red-blind) and half anomalous trichromats (red-weak). This does not alter the pattern of inheritance shown in the figure, where the two deficiency genes are lumped together.

Binomial distribution

Where a couple can produce two types of son, or two types of daughter, there is an equal probability of producing either. In the diagrams, this is shown as equal numbers of each type, e.g. in Figure 20 example (II), a normal male and carrier female are shown as producing one each of a normal male, colour-blind male, normal female and carrier female. This is a shorthand for the fact that each type of child occurs with equal probability; there is no way of knowing what you will get in advance. At conception, there is an equal chance that the child will be a boy or girl, and an equal chance that it will be normal or carry a colour deficiency gene. It is a simple matter to calculate the expected distribution between types and sexes; in statistics this is known as the **binomial distribution**. If we observed the incidence of colour deficiency in a very large number of families where there is a carrier mother with three sons, we should expect to find that 1/8 of the families had three colour defectives, 3/8 of the families had 2 colour defectives and one normal, 3/8 had 1 colour defective and 2 normal, and 1/8 of the families had 3 normally sighted sons. This is exactly the same distribution one would get by tossing a coin three times and looking at the ratio of heads and tails. What the statistics cannot do, is to provide any guarantees in an individual case. Whatever his older brothers are like, the chance of the next son showing a colour deficiency is always one half.

Female carriers

The simple picture described above shows how red-green colour deficiencies are transmitted by female carriers. A carrier has a defective red or green gene. There is a normal gene at the corresponding locus on the other X chromosome; since the normal gene is dominant over the recessive defective gene, the carrier has normal colour vision. In the case of a dual carrier, both defective genes are present, a red one on one X chromosome and a green one on the other. Since the red and green genes occupy a different locus on the chromosome, in each case the defective gene is matched by a normal gene at the corresponding locus on the other X chromosome. A dual carrier therefore has normal colour vision.

Recent investigations have shown that the situation is more complicated than the simple picture just given. Microscopic investigation of the eye shows that female carriers have a mosaic distribution of cones over their retina, combining patches of normal and defective cones. The result is that the retina contains patches with normal colour vision and patches that are colour defective. A female carrier may become aware of some slight colour deficiency when she is looking at a very small coloured object that happens to produce an image on a defective patch of the retina. When she is looking at something that produces an image on the retina large enough to overlap several patches, which is most of the time, colour vision is normal. Thus, female carriers have defective colour vision, but it is normally so slight so as to be at the limit of sensitivity of simple tests. The nature of the defect will vary with the nature of the defective gene being carried, so it is not possible to prescribe a simple colour vision test that could be used to identify the problem. General colour vision is hardly affected, and the carrier will normally pass a colour vision screening test. The mosaic pattern on the retina is equivalent to the patterned coat of a tortoiseshell cat. The gene for coat colour is carried on the cat's X chromosome. Tortoiseshells are always female. They inherit the gene for orange fur from their mother and another colour gene from their father.

In life there are exceptions to almost every rule. Individual cases have been observed and reported in the scientific literature that do not fit into the simple pattern described above. In particular, cases have been documented where a female carrier exhibits some form of colour deficient vision. From the description above this would only be expected if she were homozygous, i.e. carrying colour deficient genes on both X chromosomes. Female carriers with only one defective gene sometimes exhibit colour vision deficiency, usually mild but sometimes severe. The genetic term for this would be a manifesting heterozygote. These individuals go against the general rule that a colour defective female must have a carrier mother and a colour defective father. One case has been reported of identical female twins, where one was deuteranomalous and the other colour normal. Questions of parenthood can lead to distress and Fletcher observed *"The complexity of these matters and their sensitivity make it necessary for the non-geneticist to avoid asking too many questions"*, to which I would add *and avoid making too many assumptions*.

DNA investigations

The above description of the genetic inheritance of colour vision defects may be thought of as the classical treatment. Recent developments in genetics have enabled scientists to explore the detailed structure of individual genes and their position on the chromosome. Investigations into the genes for colour vision have shown the details to be more complicated than previously supposed, though the general picture is unaltered.

It had been suspected for some time that there were two classes of normal colour vision and this has now been confirmed by examination of the genes. For about 60% of colour normal men, the red photopigment has maximum sensitivity at a wavelength of 563 nm, while the remaining 40% have maximum sensitivity at the slightly shorter wavelength of 555 nm. This small difference is difficult to measure and the precise values of the peak wavelengths in individuals vary from measurement to measurement. The gene responsible for this variation has been identified. However, the variation is of little practical consequence.

The genes that encode for the red and green photopigments have a very similar structure to each other. This, combined with the fact that that they are situated very near to each other on the X chromosome, has resulted in a number of variations in their structure being produced over the course of human evolution. These variations have arisen during the production of new sex cells, i.e. sperm or eggs. Sperm and eggs contain 23 chromosomes, compared with the 46 (23 pairs) contained in all other body cells. Sex cells are produced in the testes and ovaries by a process known as meiosis. Each of the 23 chromosome pairs in a normal body cell derives one member of the pair from the mother and the other from the father. In meiosis, the two are rearranged to produce a new single chromosome, containing characteristics of both parents. This chromosome becomes one of the 23 chromosomes contained in the new sex cell. The sex cell, or gamete, is either a sperm or egg, as appropriate to the person. The sex cell will later combine with its counterpart during fertilisation to produce an offspring.

During meiosis in a female cell, a process called crossing over may take place. This involves the two X chromosomes swapping sections of the chromosome between them. The point along the chromosome at which the break and rearrangement takes place is variable. On the X chromosome, the genes for red and green photopigments are similar in structure to each other and sit at nearby loci on the chromosome. If the crossing over occurs at the location of the genes for colour pigments, the resulting gamete may end up with a rather muddled arrangement of the genes. A gene may be slightly displaced along the DNA molecule, or perhaps an extra copy of the gene is acquired. Another situation that can arise is the formation of a hybrid gene. Hybrid genes are variously known by different authors as chimeric, hybrid or fusion genes. The words emphasise the fact that the variant genes are formed from a combination of the normal red and green genes.

This crossover event has produced a new colour deficient gene in the sex cell. If the cell is subsequently fertilised, the defect will be passed on to future generations; a new family line has been created that will contain colour defective members. Many subtle combinations of displaced and hybrid genes are possible. This explains the range of red-green defects that are observed in practice. Modern techniques have allowed a detailed description of the genetics of colour vision; the interested reader is referred to the bibliography for more information.

Detailed investigations of the relation between the chimeric genes and colour vision defects have changed the description of the weak form of colour blindness. A red-weak (protanomalous) defective has up to now been considered as having a normal gene for the green photopigment, and a modified red gene that shifts the peak wavelength response towards the green. The new work has shown that the red-weak defective chromosome is more properly considered as lacking the red gene, and possessing two forms of green: a normal green photopigment gene, plus a modified green photopigment whose peak sensitivity is shifted towards the red. This conceptual change has no practical consequence. Whether the long wave pigment of a red-weak person is considered as a green pigment displaced towards red, or a red displaced towards green, need not concern us further.

A most interesting development is that it is now possible to carry out a genetic test for colour vision. Conventional colour vision screening tests are not very good at identifying the type or severity of a colour vision defect, nor can they be used with young children. A genetic test, performed on drop of blood from the subject, can identify most defects with great accuracy. It should also be of great value when dealing with a person who simultaneously has both acquired and inherited colour vision problems, where conventional tests have difficulty in separating the different causes.

Achromatopsia

There is a very rare disorder termed **atypical achromatopsia**. The sufferer has normal visual acuity and an ophthalmic examination of the retina appears to show normally functioning cones and no other eye defects. However, there is a gross, usually complete, loss of colour perception. It is thought that the loss of colour sensation occurs at a higher level than the retina. The eye operates normally and sends the appropriate signal up the optic nerve to the brain. Somehow, the brain fails to process the signals and does not produce any colour sensation; this is reflected in an alternative name for the condition, **cerebral achromatopsia**. The defect is extremely rare, perhaps 1 in 10 million people, and few cases have been investigated. It is not inherited and may result from trauma or illness. It will not be considered further in this book.

Congenital achromatopsia is a rare congenital disorder in which the person is lacking in cone vision and relies on rods for all sight, hence the alternative name of **rod monochromatism.** As was described in the last chapter, rods are responsible for night vision. In daylight or other bright light, rod vision is disabled when the visual pigment is bleached. Achromats, as the sufferers are termed, are therefore totally colour-blind and have poor vision in bright light, making the wearing of dark glasses essential both outdoors and in well-lit interiors. The central area of the macula, normally used for detailed sight, is lacking in the achromatic eye. The achromat develops involuntary eye movements or **nystagmus,** which move the image off-centre to the area of the retina containing the rods. Visual acuity is well below normal. Variations are termed **cone monochromatism** or **incomplete achromatopsia,** where sufferers appear to have some residual cone function, which gives them a slight colour sense. This is not fully understood and does little to improve overall visual performance.

Acquired defects

Acquired colour vision defects are more common than is generally realised. It has been said that at least 5% of the population have an acquired defect as severe as the 8% with a congenital defect. A disturbance to normal colour vision can occur as a result of

- disease - either in the eye itself or a more general condition
- injury - usually to the eye or head
- exposure to chemicals or medication
- age

Acquired defects show a wide range of characteristics, making simple classification difficult. They are distinguished from inherited characteristics in a number of ways, set out in *Table 11*.

Table 11. **Inherited and acquired defects**	
Inherited	**Acquired**
Present from birth	Appear later in life
Permanent and unchanging	Severity may fluctuate or be reversible
Limited range of defects	Many variations of defect found; hard to classify
Both eyes the same	The eyes may differ from each other
Normal visual acuity	Visual acuity often affected. Other deficiencies include impaired dark adaptation, nystagmus and changes in the visual field
Predominantly found in males	Found in both males and females
Predominantly red-green defects	Often a blue defect

The range of acquired defects is large and the list of possible causes even greater. No attempt will be made to provide a comprehensive list in this book. Some of the major causes are summarised below.

- **Glaucoma** is a condition in which the pressure of the fluid in the eyeball is raised. The level may be high enough to compress the blood vessels at the back of the eye that supply the optic nerve. The majority of people with chronic simple glaucoma show a deficiency in blue-yellow perception. The defect is often found in only one eye. A loss in colour vision may be the first indication of the onset of glaucoma and so could be used in diagnosis.

- **Diabetes** may cause retinopathy. Blue colour deficiencies are associated with diabetic retinopathy. Colour vision tests may be used to detect the onset of retinopathy and to indicate whether the patient should be referred for a detailed ophthalmic investigation, which would tell whether further treatment was required.

- **Injury.** There are many recorded cases of severe colour disturbance following a blow to the front or back of the head. The changes in perception may be transient or permanent. In some cases, colour vision may not be fully restored until some years have elapsed since the original injury.

- **Age.** The crystalline lens of the eye becomes less transparent with age. The lens absorbs more blue light, giving the lens a slightly yellow appearance. The result is that blue-weak colour deficiencies begin to appear from the age of 30 or 40 onwards. They are rarely serious enough to lead to a diagnosis of colour vision deficiency.

- **Chemicals** and **drugs** may damage the visual system. Any substances that cause damage to the visual system will almost inevitably affect colour vision at the same time as producing a range of other visual effects. However, such substances are either drugs or known poisons and inadvertent exposure should not occur.

- **Heavy tobacco smoking**, aggravated by the consumption of alcohol, can produce the condition of tobacco amblyopia. This typically take the form of a red-green disturbance similar to red-weak inherited colour deficiencies.

Summary: Colour blindness

By far the most common forms of colour vision deficiency are the various types of red-green colour blindness. Some 8% of European males have a deficiency, and about 0.5% of females. The most common inheritance is from grandfather to grandson; the mother carries the genes for the deficiency, but seldom experiences it.

Colour blindness has various types and degrees of severity, depending on which of the three types of cone photoreceptor in the eye are affected and the nature of the defect.

- Red and green-blind people are classed as dichromats.

- Red-blind people are lacking cone photopigment in the eye that is most sensitive to red light (long wave or L pigment).

- Green-blind people are lacking the cone photopigment in the eye that is most sensitive to green light (middle wave or M cone).

- Dichromacy is the most severe form of red-green colour blindness and affects about 2% of males. Both types of dichromats have similar problems. The range of colours from green, though yellow and orange, to red are seen as the same, differing only in lightness and saturation. Grey is indistinguishable from blue-green. Red-blind people see dark red as virtually black and are worse than green-blind people in distinguishing among different shades of purple.

People with the weak form of colour vision deficiency are termed anomalous trichromats.

- Red-weak people have normal green cones, but the response of their red cones is "greener" than normal, giving reduced sensitivity to red light.

- Green-weak people have normal red cones, but the response of their green cones is "redder" than normal, giving reduced sensitivity to green light.

- A wide range of severity of anomalous defects is found. The severity may be measured by the difference in wavelength between the peak sensitivity of the red and green cone photopigments. For normal colour vision, the figure is 30 nm. For those with anomalous colour vision, the difference may be as low as 1 nm, or up to nearly 30 nm. Thus people classified as "colour-blind" may have nearly normal colour vision, or any intermediate degree up to nearly a dichromat. Those with a mild form of colour deficiency may be able to distinguish between red and green, but have problems with pastel colours or dark unsaturated colours such as brown and olive green.

Other inherited forms of colour vision deficiency are rare. They include tritanopia, where the blue cones are absent or abnormal, and the class of defects known as achromatopsia, where colour vision is completely lacking. It is also possible to acquire colour vision deficiency later in life. This results from the effects of disease or exposure to drugs or chemicals. Acquired defects often affect the perception of blue and so are different from the common inherited deficiency.

Chapter 4 - Diagnosis

A diagnosis of the type and severity of a colour vision deficiency can be of great assistance to the individual and their family. It can help explain any difficulties and confusions that have been experienced. An early and realistic assessment of the effect of colour vision deficiency on possible careers will help in making appropriate choices. This may avoid disappointment later on, not to say the potential waste of time in following an inappropriate course of study. Evidence of superior ability to discriminate or remember colours is a positive qualification for some jobs. Some colour vision tests can be used to grade normal colour vision and assist in identifying those with above average colour ability.

The ideal diagnostic test would give information on:

- Type: what is the type of any deficiency, red, green or blue? Is the defect congenital or has it been acquired as a result of disease or some other cause?

- Severity: how severe is the defect? Is the person a dichromat, totally lacking one colour class of photopigments, or do they have a milder, anomalous, form of colour vision defect? If so, is the defect severe, moderate or mild?

- Implications: what are the implications for the person? Are any careers or activities impossible or inadvisable? If the defect is acquired, are there medical implications requiring referral for further investigation?

The testing of colour vision requires a lot more subtlety than simply asking the subject to identify and name some colours. Every colour-blind person knows that if they mention their problem, they will be subjected to a barrage of questions of the "What colour socks am I wearing?" variety. Colour naming is an inadequate test for colour vision deficiency. Young children may not yet have learn't colour names satisfactorily. A mild deficiency may have interfered with satisfactory learning of colour names, so that they can in fact discriminate colours better than would be indicated by their fluency in using the colour names. There are also language problems. Chapter 2 described how colour names do not always translate directly between different languages. Situations where the subject has a mother tongue different from that of the tester could cause difficulties. On the other hand, by adulthood, the colour defective will have learnt by experience to use all possible cues to assist in guessing the colour of an object. Appearance cues such as texture and shininess often help. Above all, the use of colour names by normally sighted people leads to associations between objects and colours. Green and grass go together as do blood and red, and no colour defective is likely to describe a lawn as red - though they might have difficulty naming the colour correctly if it were presented as an isolated coloured patch of light on a screen. Royal Mail pillar boxes will always be named red and grass green without hesitation. However, when it comes to a pepper or tomato, which can be either red or green, there may be problems. The first tests for faulty colour vision were indeed colour naming tests. John Dalton used a set of 20 coloured ribbons in his investigations. However, such tests have now been discarded in favour of more reliable methods.

Types of test

When acquired defects are included, there is quite a wide range of different types of defective colour vision and it is impossible for a single test to give a complete diagnosis. In practice, a battery of tests is used. The most familiar type of test is the **pseudoisochromatic plate**, the most widely used example of which is the Ishihara test. This is the test most likely to be met when a routine colour vision screening test is given, perhaps at an eye test or school medical. The test consists of a series of printed coloured plates. Each plate is made up of irregular coloured dots, which conceal a hidden figure, typically a numeral. The figure can easily be seen by colour normals, but not by the colour deficient. This type of test can be used to give a rapid screening to differentiate between normal and defective colour vision and can also be used to distinguish between those with red and green colour deficiencies. The test gives no indication of severity, nor will it detect blue deficiencies.

The typical **arrangement test** consists of a set of coloured discs, usually known as caps, rather like a set of draughts pieces with a range of coloured tops. The colours change from one cap to the next in a series of small steps. The caps are shuffled and the subject is then asked to place them in order in a box. The starting cap is fixed and the subject is asked to choose the cap that is closest to it in colour and place it next to the start. This is repeated until all the caps have been placed in a row. The order that the caps are placed in can be scored to give a measure of how serious any colour vision defect may be. In one of the common tests, the colour steps between the caps are sufficiently small so that a person with normal colour vision will make some errors. An unusually low error score is evidence of a superior level of colour discrimination ability.

The **anomaloscope** is used to classify and grade red-green defects. It is a piece of optical equipment that can mix red and green lights in various proportions, while keeping the overall brightness constant. The subject looks into an eyepiece and can see the mixture of red and green lights, compared side by side with a monochromatic yellow light. The subject is asked to vary the mixture of red and green lights and the brightness of the yellow light, until both halves of the visual field look the same. People with normal colour vision all produce more or less the same proportion of red and green to match the yellow. Those with a red-weak deficiency require a higher proportion of red light, while those with a green-weak deficiency require extra green. Dichromats manage some sort of match with virtually any proportion of red and green, but will need to alter the brightness of the yellow light to light to get a match. This test is the most important tool for investigating red-green deficiencies.

Lantern tests are prescribed for some occupational examinations, since they have high face validity, i.e. they try and test the ability that will be needed in the actual job. A lantern fitted with a set of colour filters is used to present signal colours. The subject is asked to name the colours, which are chosen to represent those used in rail and traffic signals.

Computer-based tests are being developed in several laboratories and have many advantages. A wide range of test material can be presented on the monitor; presentation and scoring can be automated. Some computer tests are based on conventional diagnostic tests while others have been specially developed to exploit the potential of the new medium. A reliable computer test demands a carefully calibrated and consistent colour monitor and perhaps for this reason they have not become widely used outside the research laboratory. Examples of such tests may be found on the World Wide Web and some sites are suggested in the bibliography.

Pseudoisochromatic tests

This type of test consists of a set of diagrams, each of which is composed of coloured dots. When looked at by a colour normal, a coloured symbol can be seen to stand out against the background. The symbol is some easily identified figure, such as an Arabic numeral, or simple geometrical figure, such as triangle or circle. Isochromatic means "of the same colour" and the pseudo prefix means that dots are chosen to look the same colour to the colour deficient, but not to the colour normal. In this way, the normal and the deficient see a different figure and the difference is independent of any ability to name colours.

The pseudoisochromatic plates aim to remove all visual cues other than colour itself. By using a background of dots with varying size and brightness, the effects of shape and lightness are removed, so that the only way the embedded figure can be distinguished from the background is by the colour, or more strictly the hue, of the dots composing it.

This is analogous to the problem of the primeval ape searching for ripe fruit among the leaves of the forest, which, it is supposed, drove the evolution of colour vision.

Pseudoisochromatic plates test the ability of subjects to distinguish low colour contrast shapes in the presence other high contrasts. There is a recently recognised condition known as the Meares-Irlen syndrome. People with this syndrome suffer from a form of visual stress when looking at a visual field that contains high contrasts. They often suffer from a form of dyslexia that may be helped by reading through a coloured overlay or by wearing tinted glasses. They are occasionally wrongly diagnosed as colour deficient as a result of poor performance on a pseudoisochromatic test, even though they perform other tests of colour discrimination such as the FM 100 arrangement test perfectly well.

Printed pseudoisochromatic plates are the most widely used method of screening for colour vision deficiencies. Many versions have been produced throughout the world of varying quality. Coloured diagrams are now easy to set up on colour computer monitors and examples of pseudoisochromatic tests have proliferated on the World Wide Web. Five minutes with a search engine will throw up a dozen or so examples. However, a proper assessment of colour vision deficiency requires that the test plates be reproduced to a high and consistent standard. Only two are in worldwide use, the Ishihara plates and the American Optical Hardy, Rand and Rittler plates; the latter known commonly by the abbreviation HRR. A specialised set of pseudoisochromatic plates, the City University tritan test, is used when it is desired to test for the range of blue (tritan) deficiencies.

The Ishihara test plates
The Ishihara pseudoisochromatic test was designed in Japan as long ago as 1917 and is the most widely used test in the UK. It has gone through many reprintings and is available in several different editions The full Ishihara test consists of 38 plates; an abbreviated edition of 24 and a concise edition of 14 plates are available. They include the following types of plate:

- Vanishing designs. A number can be seen by people with normal colour vision, but cannot be seen by the colour deficient. All the dots are chosen from the region of orange, yellow and yellow-green where both red and green deficient people have similar confusions. Referring back to the chromaticity diagram of Figure 17, this is the region where the confusion lines for red-blind and green-blind are similar.

- Transformation designs. A number is seen by people with normal colour vision and a different one by colour deficient observers.

- Hidden digit design. A number can be seen by the colour deficient but not by those with normal vision.

- Classification. Plates designed to distinguish between red deficient and green deficient vision. They are of vanishing design. Normals can see two numbers. People with a red deficiency can see one and those with a green deficiency the other.

The complete test set contains additional plates based on the same principles, but using shapes rather than numerals. These are designed for children or non-literate subjects and the subject responds by tracing the shape that is visible to them. The Ishihara plates are very effective in distinguishing between normals and those with a red-green deficiency. They cannot, and are not designed to, detect blue deficiencies. For maximum effectiveness the plates should be used under the correct conditions, with a viewing distance of 75cm and daylight illumination. A daylight fluorescent light is satisfactory, but an illuminant with a high proportion of red light, such as a tungsten lamp, may reduce the number of errors made by a colour deficient subject. Each plate should be viewed for about 4 seconds. If the subject is allowed to handle the plates and take their time, they can improve their score by such tactics as varying the illumination by moving the plate under the light. The figures to be identified are composed of dots of varying size and have a rather broken appearance. This can lead to errors such as naming a 5 as a 6. Such partial errors do not affect the outcome of the test, which has shown itself to be very reliable. The plates are printed to a high standard and will maintain their accuracy if kept closed when not in use and touching the surface of the plates is avoided.

The Ishihara test is readily available and is the most widely used test for screening for colour vision deficiency. Some sample plates are reproduced in **Figure 22** (see page 69). Its wide distribution and apparent simplicity means that it is often administered by testers with little experience or understanding of the proper test methods. Wide differences have been reported in the results obtained with Ishihara tests used by school nurses in England. For reliable results, it is most important that the correct test procedures are followed.

HRR plates
These plates were first produced by the American Optical Co. in 1954. The test contains 24 plates of the vanishing type. The plates consist of a background of coloured circles with a range of size and lightness, among which are hidden geometric symbols. These are made up of circles with colours designed to be difficult to detect by those with a colour deficiency. The symbols are a cross, a circle and a triangle, and it is the task of the subject under test to say what symbol is present. The first four plates shown to the subject are demonstration plates; this demonstrates the form of the test and the symbols are readily visible. Failure to identify the figures indicates possible malingering or other problems on

the part of the subject. Successive plates identify the type of colour vision defect, if any, and also give a measure of severity. The Ishihara and the HRR plates are often used together in a clinical examination. The Ishihara plates are used as an effective and sensitive screening for a red-green defect. The HRR plates indicate the severity of any defect and will also screen for a tritan defect.

The City University tritan test

Since the Ishihara test does not identify blue colour deficiency an additional test may be needed. The City University tritan test is designed to supplement the Ishihara test when it is desired to test for tritan defects. It contains five plates of the vanishing type, i.e. the designs can be seen by normals but not by the blue deficient. Three plates are used to screen for the existence of a defect and the other two to grade the severity of the defect. All designs are simple geometrical shapes, rather than the numbers of the Ishihara test. The plates successfully screen for congenital tritan defects and have been used extensively in the study of acquired colour deficiency in diabetics.

The City University test

The City University Colour Vision Test, not to be confused with the City University tritan test, consists of ten plates. Each plate is printed on a black background and consists of five coloured circles. They are arranged as a central disc surrounded by four peripheral colours. The subject is asked to identify the peripheral colour that most nearly matches the central colour. The test is derived from the D15 test and employs the same selection of colours. In each plate, one of the peripheral colours is the adjacent colour to the central colour in the D15 sequence; this makes it the expected choice for a colour normal. The other three peripheral colours represent typical protan, deutan and tritan confusions. The scoring system set out in the test manual allows the type and severity of any colour deficiency to be assessed. The City University Colour Vision Test is not an effective screening test; some subjects will pass who would be classified as colour deficient by the Ishihara test. It gives information on the severity of any defect and distinguishes between red-weak and green-weak deficiencies, though not with total reliability. It is the most widely used test that will pick out the tritan (blue-weak) family of deficiencies. The test is illustrated in **Figure 23** (see page 72).

Reproduction plates

Examples of pseudoisochromatic plates are widely reproduced, in magazines and books, including this one. Examples are available for use on a computer screen. The Internet can be used to locate several web sites that display colour vision tests, some hosted by academic departments, others by manufacturers of colour correcting lenses. Using a search engine to look for "colour vision deficiency" will rapidly find a few examples. A word of caution is needed. The standard tests are printed to a high and reproducible quality and for consistent results should be used by a trained tester under standard conditions. A plate printed in a magazine or book, or an image transmitted over the Internet, cannot be relied on to provide an accurate test. Have fun with them by all means, but the results should not be used to provide a diagnosis that may result in important decisions.

Arrangement tests

Arrangement tests require the subject to place a series of coloured caps in sequential order of colour. I will use the word subject for the person taking the test: patient makes them sound ill, while testee is too American. One colour is fixed in position as the start. There are two widely used tests of this sort, both of which were developed by Dean Farnsworth in 1943. They are known as the Farnsworth D15 test, with 15 colours to be sorted, and the Farnsworth-Munsell 100 Hue Test. The names are commonly abbreviated to the D15 and the FM100. The original purpose of the tests was for vocational selection and guidance; the D15 test was actually devised for use by a transformer company to assist in the selection of electricians.

Both tests consist of a series of caps each containing a coloured disc of about 13 mm diameter. A photograph of the FM 100 test is shown in **Figure 24** (see page 121). To carry out the test, the examiner shuffles the caps face up on a table and asks the subject to place them in a row in their wooden box so that they form a sequence of colours. The subject selects the cap that is closest in colour to the fixed starting cap and places it next to the starting cap. They continue in this manner until all caps have been placed in a continuous, natural looking, sequence. The different basis of the two tests may be explained using the chromaticity diagram. Both tests contain a set of colours that form a complete colour circle, i.e. they cover the whole range of spectral colours from red to blue and complete the circle with purples. All the colours have the same saturation and lightness. This is important, to prevent a colour deficient subject from making a selection based on perceived difference in lightness instead of colour alone. The D15 test uses 15 moveable colours plus a fixed starting or 'pilot' colour. Subjects with colour vision deficiency will tend to confuse colours on opposite sides of the colour circle; which colours are confused depends on the type of defect. The FM100 test originally had 100 colours, but the number was later reduced to 85 colours. The colour difference between adjacent caps is now very small, equivalent to a difference in the wavelength of the characteristic spectral colour of less than 3 nm. The small difference means that people with

Figure 1. The visible spectrum

Modern colour names are shown.

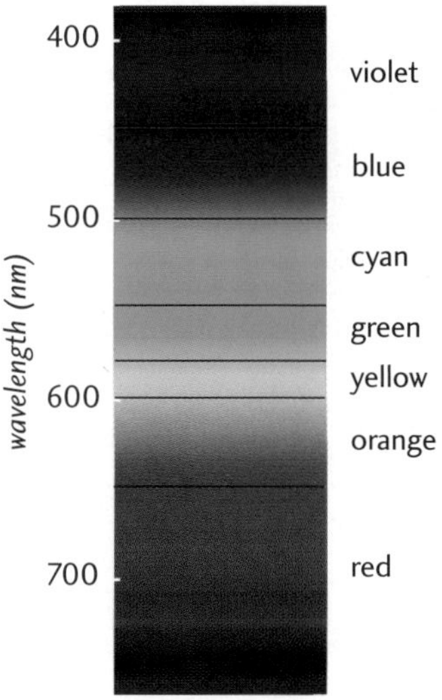

wavelength (nm)

400 — violet

blue

500 — cyan

green

600 — yellow

orange

700 — red

Figure 5. Colour wheel

Opposite colours are complementary and add to produce white.

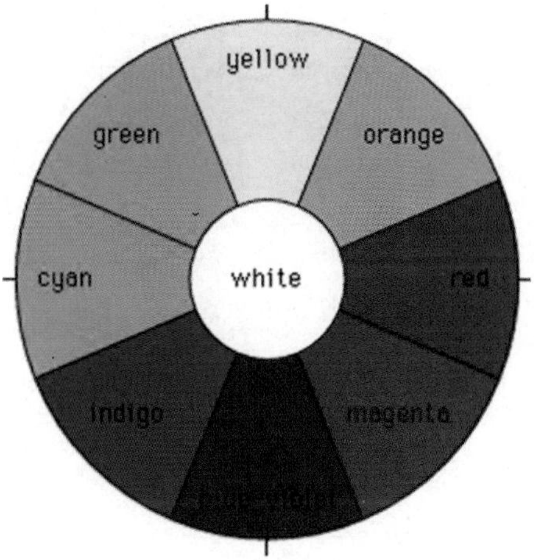

yellow
green
orange
cyan
white
red
indigo
magenta
blue-violet

Figure 4. Colour mixing

(a) additive mixing - lights
(b) subtractive mixing - paints

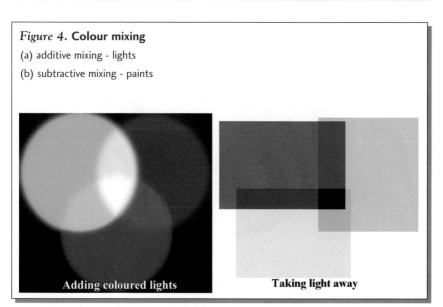

Adding coloured lights

Taking light away

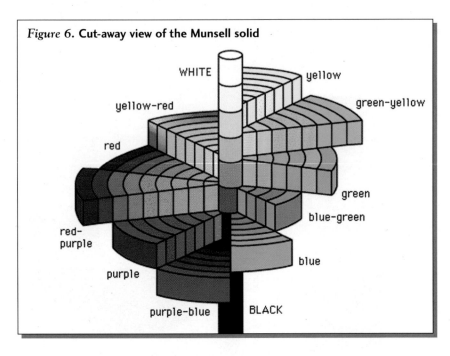

Figure 6. **Cut-away view of the Munsell solid**

WHITE

yellow

yellow-red

green-yellow

red

green

blue-green

red-purple

blue

purple

purple-blue

BLACK

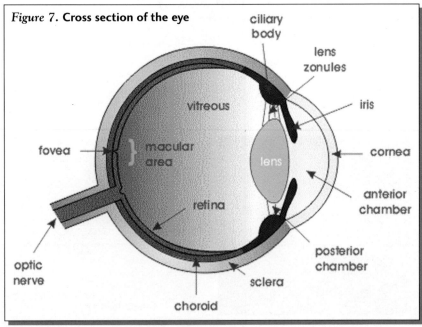

Figure 7. **Cross section of the eye**

ciliary body

lens zonules

vitreous

iris

fovea

macular area

cornea

lens

optic nerve

retina

anterior chamber

posterior chamber

sclera

choroid

Figure 12. **Ripe fruit among green leaves**

The second photograph has been altered to show how the tree appears to a person or ape lacking red photopigment.

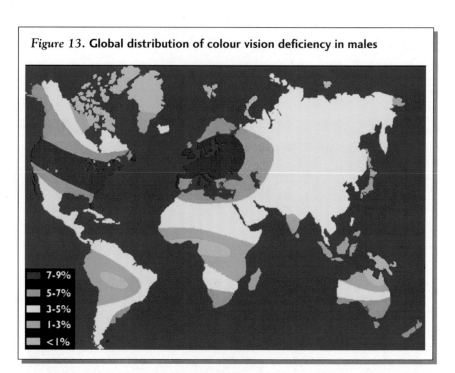

Figure 13. Global distribution of colour vision deficiency in males

7-9%
5-7%
3-5%
1-3%
<1%

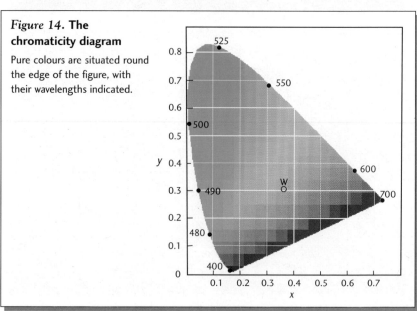

Figure 14. The chromaticity diagram

Pure colours are situated round the edge of the figure, with their wavelengths indicated.

Figure 22. Examples of Ishihara test plates

In Plate 1, everyone should see the figure 12. In Plate 2, colour normals see a 8, while red-green defectives see 3. In plate 6 the figures are 15 and 17 for normals and defectives.

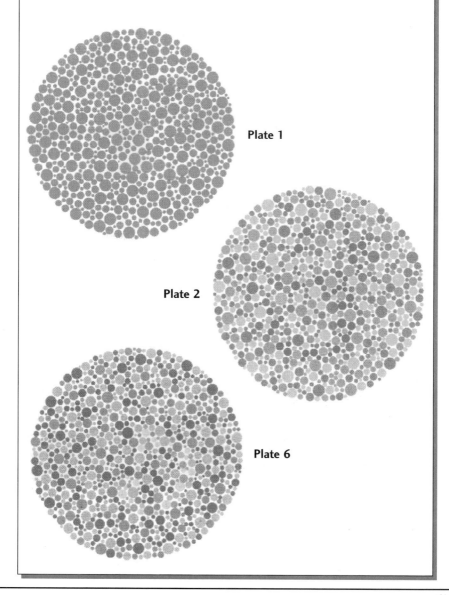

Plate 1

Plate 2

Plate 6

Figure 20. Patterns of inheritance (single defect)

I.   The pattern starts with a colour defective father and a normal mother. All daughters are carriers and all sons are normal.

II. A normal father and carrier mother produce both normal and carrier daughters, and both normal and defective sons.

III. A colour defective father and a carrier mother produce both carrier and colour defective daughters, and both normal and colour defective sons.

IV. A normal father and colour defective mother produce all colour defective sons and all carrier daughters.

V.   A colour defective father and colour defective mother produce all colour defective sons and all colour defective daughters.

VI. Similar to II, showing that the origin of colour deficiency in a male may extend further back than the maternal grandfather: in this case it started with the great-grandfather.

In all cases where parents produce two types of son or daughter, each occurs with equal probability.

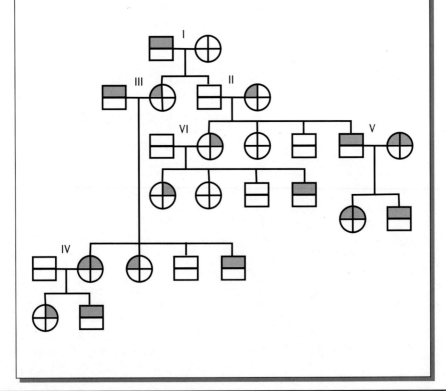

Figure 21. Patterns of inheritance (mixed defects)

I. A red defective father and a green carrier mother produce both normal and green defective sons, and both red deficiency carrier and dual carrier daughters.

II. A red defective father and a dual carrier mother produce both red defective and green defective sons, and both red defective and dual carrier daughters.

III. A green defective father and a red defective mother produce red defective sons and dual carrier daughters.

IV. A normal father and dual carrier mother produce both red and green defective sons, and green and red deficiency carrier daughters.

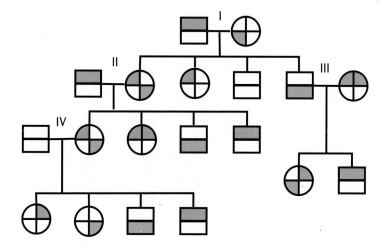

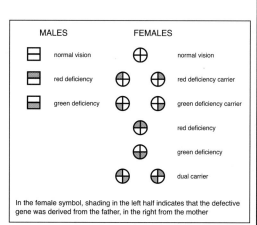

MALES		FEMALES	
	normal vision		normal vision
	red deficiency		red deficiency carrier
	green deficiency		green deficiency carrier
			red deficiency
			green deficiency
			dual carrier

In the female symbol, shading in the left half indicates that the defective gene was derived from the father, in the right from the mother

Figure 23. The City University Colour Vision Test.

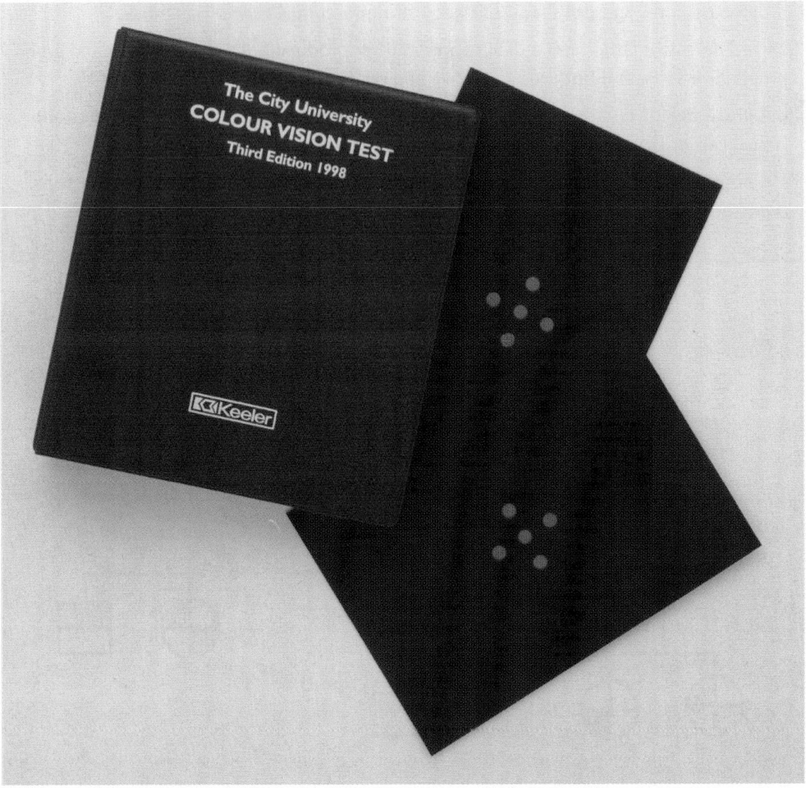

normal colour vision will inevitably make some errors in placing the caps and the test can be used to identify people with superior colour discrimination. The large number of caps in a FM100 test requires the test to be given in four separate boxes. Colours from opposite sides of the colour circle are not presented together, so that confusions of opposite colours do not occur. Colour deficient subjects will show maximum errors on this test in regions where their isochromatic confusion zones are tangential to the colour circle in the chromaticity diagram. This occurs in different regions for the different type of deficiency. The arrangement tests are always presented by a trained tester, who is responsible for the proper administration, scoring and interpretation. They are not suitable for DIY testing.

D15 scoring
The D15 test was originally designed to classify people into two groups. The first group contains those with normal colour vision and slight colour deficiency. The second contains those with moderate and severe colour deficiency. A single error of two steps or more is classed as a fail. The pass criterion includes people with normal colour vision and those with only a slight colour deficiency. About 5% of males fail the test, compared with the total of 8% with some form of deficiency. The test was designed for employment selection and those who pass are considered to be able to use industrial colour codes safely. By plotting the response of the subject on a circular diagram, it is possible for the tester to diagnose the type of colour deficiency, i.e. blue, green or red, by noting the confusions. Scoring methods have been developed which give a more sensitive measure of severity of defect than the original pass-fail criterion.

FM100 scoring
The results of the FM100 test are analysed by the tester to give an overall performance score. The total error score gives an overall figure of merit for hue discrimination, but is of no diagnostic value as to the type of colour vision deficiency. To provide information on the type of colour defect, the scores are plotted on a polar diagram; interpretation of this diagram requires training and experience and is left to the expert. The colour separation between adjacent discs is small and colour normals make errors. The errors are most frequent in the blue-green region, which is where the colour separations are smallest. This region of the spectrum is also the region where colour discrimination deteriorates with age. Performance on the FM100 test therefore shows a marked decline with age, as is shown in *Figure 25*. The data for this figure was obtained using a set of tests conducted under a relatively low lighting level, below the standard usually employed in the test. The error scores in the diagram are therefore rather higher than usually found and exaggerate the decline in discrimination for the older subjects.

Many factors affect the results of the FM100 test. The effect of illumination has already been mentioned; low illumination levels increase the error score, especially with older subjects. A subject can improve their performance by taking extra care and time to distinguish small differences; the tester usually allows the subject to rearrange the discs to get the best possible sequence. It is found that performance may improve by up to 30% when the test is taken a second time. The discs have been carefully designed to have all

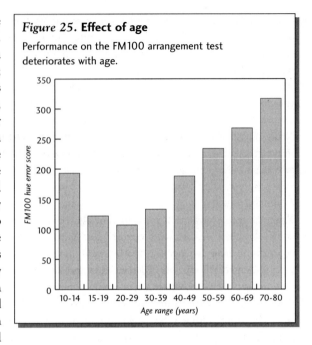

Figure 25. **Effect of age**

Performance on the FM100 arrangement test deteriorates with age.

the same lightness to eliminate any cues other than colour. However, subjects with poor red vision will find that discs at the red end of the range appear darker to them. Red-blind subjects therefore achieve higher scores than might otherwise be expected since they tend to use lightness as an additional cue when sorting the discs. The overall FM100 score is therefore not a sufficient indicator of the disability the subject may find when carrying out real-world tasks. Interpretation of the FM100 test therefore requires both skill and experience. It should not be used on its own and is unsatisfactory as a screening test. It was originally intended that subjects should be classified only in three categories: superior, average and inferior colour discrimination.

The anomaloscope

One of the basic additive colour mixes is that red and green lights mixed together produce yellow. As might be expected, people with a red-green colour deficiency produce a different mix from normals. This test is known as the Rayleigh match. This forms the basis of the **anomaloscope**, which produces a quantitative measure of the type and degree of a red-green deficiency. The most commonly used is the Nagel anomaloscope, illustrated in *Figure 26* (see page 121). The subject looks into a viewing hood and sees a circular illuminated area, divided into two halves. One half is illuminated with pure yellow light and the other half by a mixture of red and green. The subject may adjust the brightness of the yellow light and the proportions of red and green in the mix; the device is arranged so that the brightness of the mixture stays constant as the proportions are changed. It is possible to construct an anomaloscope for demonstration or laboratory purposes using coloured filters to produce the coloured illumination. Better results are obtained using monochromatic light and the standard clinical instruments used for diagnosis use the monochromatic wavelengths of 589 nm (sodium yellow), 546 nm (mercury green) and 670 nm (lithium red) as stimuli. This combination of red and green mixes to give a saturated yellow that can be accurately matched by a colour normal to the monochromatic sodium yellow.

The subject is first asked to produce the best match possible between the two halves of the field by adjusting both knobs, i.e. altering both the brightness of the yellow field and the proportions of red and green in the mix. The tester does not use colour names, but says words to the effect "Alter both the control wheels until the two halves of the circle look exactly the same colour and the same brightness". The subject repeats this a few times, with a short rest in between. The next part of the test finds out the limits of the matching range. People with normal colour vision can produce a match with a consistent ratio of red and green. People with progressively poorer colour vision will accept a wider range of mixtures as an acceptable match and the limits of the range provide valuable information on the nature of the deficiency. The tester now sets the red-green ratio in steps and the subject tries to obtain a match by adjusting the yellow brightness control only. The tester says "I have set one half of the field of view. See if you can obtain an exact match by altering this wheel only. Please answer 'Yes, I can match the two halves of the circle exactly' or 'No, I cannot'". This test is repeated to obtain the limits of the matching range, i.e. the maximum and minimum red-green ratios that the subject can match to yellow.

On the conventional Nagel anomaloscope, the mixture scale runs from 0 (pure green) to 73 (pure red). Subjects with normal colour vision produce a match with a mean value of 42 and a matching range of 5. This means that a normal subject will accept red-green mixtures from 40 to 45 as matching yellow; the actual numbers will vary slightly from individual to individual and between tests for a single individual. Some people are much more consistent than others in reproducing the colour match from test to test; the range varies from 1 to 10 scale units. People with normal colour vision, but who have a matching range that is more than twice the modal value of the general population may be classified as colour weak.

There have been some attempts to introduce an improved measurement scale, which among other things would allow direct comparisons between measurements made on different instruments. The anomaly quotient, also known as the anomalquotient (AQ), was defined as the subject's green/red ratio divided by the standard green/red ratio. For example, a red-weak subject who produces a match at 50 has an anomaly quotient

$$AQ = ((73-50)/50)/((73-42)/42) = 0.62$$

Colour normals produce mean AQ scores of near to unity, with a matching range of about 0.2. Red-weak subjects produce AQs of less than unity, green-weak of greater than unity. The AQ scale is unsatisfactory for subjects with severe colour deficiency and has not been widely adopted.

Dichromats are lacking one of the photopigments and will accept *any* mixture of red and green as providing an acceptable match to yellow. However, changing the red-green mixture produces a variation in perceived brightness. The red-blind subject will see the brightness of the mixture reduce as the proportion of red is increased and so will reduce the brightness of the yellow to maintain a match. Those subjects with a red or green weakness accept a matching range that is displaced to one side of the normal. As would be expected, the green-weak require additional green in the matching mixture and the red-weak require extra red. Increased levels of defect increase the width of the matching range.

Figure 27 illustrates the range of matches that are produced by subjects with various types of colour vision. Colour normals produce results close to the mean normal match. Both green-blind and red-blind subjects will accept any combination of red and green as a match to yellow. However the red-blind subject will see the brightness of the mixture vary according to the proportions of red and green. If the mixture contains a high proportion of red, the mix is

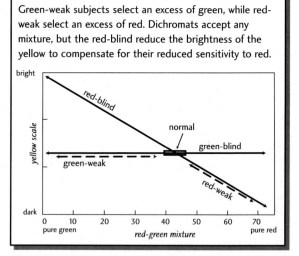

Figure 27. **Anomaloscope matching ranges**
Green-weak subjects select an excess of green, while red-weak select an excess of red. Dichromats accept any mixture, but the red-blind reduce the brightness of the yellow to compensate for their reduced sensitivity to red.

seen as dim and the brightness of the yellow matching field has to be reduced to compensate. The green-blind subject accepts any mixture as a match, with little variation in brightness. As would be expected, red-weak subjects require more red in the mix to produce a match to yellow and also reduce the yellow brightness to compensate. Green-weak subjects require a higher proportion of green. Neither green-weak nor red-weak persons accept the normal match and the distance of the match from normal is an indication of the severity of their deficiency.

The anomaloscope is the only clinical instrument that can provide an accurate diagnosis of the range of red-green colour deficiencies. The instrument is expensive and requires a trained and experienced operator. There are several variations of the anomaloscope to be found other than the Nagel. One type offers a Moreland match, rather than the common Rayleigh match. The Moreland match requires the subject to match a fixed mix of cyan and yellow, with a variable mixture of blue and green. This instrument was developed for the investigation of acquired colour deficiencies.

Lanterns

The safety implications of poor colour vision arose first over the use of coloured signal lanterns on the railways and navigation lights on ships at sea. Asking a subject to name the colour of a signal light provides a test of high practical value, even though it may not reveal much of the nature and severity of any colour defect. However, the tests are robust and have the advantage of testing the required ability directly. Lantern tests are used in most countries as part of the vision requirements for pilots, railway workers and seamen. The basic form of the lantern test is that the subject is shown a number of signal lights and asked to name them. The colours are chosen to represent standard signal colours. It is important that the lantern tests are administered strictly according to the test protocols. Changes in brightness, viewing distance or viewing time may alter the results in marginal cases. In most cases, the subject wants to pass the test; their job may depend on it. The subject will therefore use every cue available to help guess at the correct answer. Those with a red deficiency will already know from their own experience that reds appear very dark and so if the test signal appears very dark, or invisible, the colour is best guessed as red. Random guessing between red and green will produce the right answer half the time. The tests therefore give repeated presentations of the signal colours and any single misnaming of red or green is sufficient to count as a failure.

The advantages of the lantern tests may be summarised:

- A practical and realistic trade test, which accepts those capable of a reliable performance, even if they have a slight colour vision deficiency.

- A convincing test. A demonstration of the inability to name the signal colours should convince any colour normal friend or advocate that the subject should be rejected for critical employment.

The Ishihara plates are very sensitive in detecting those with a red or green colour vision deficiency. Reliance on them alone would result in the rejection of candidates for jobs where their degree of defect would not present a practical difficulty. The sensitivities of the Ishihara plates, a lantern test and the D15 test are compared in **Table 12**, which shows that the lantern test is effective in passing those with a mild but acceptable defect.

Table 12. **Comparison of test sensitivities**

Degree of deficiency	Ishihara	Lantern	D15
Normal	Pass	Pass	Pass
Mild (safe)	Fail	Pass	Pass
Medium	Fail	Fail	Pass
Severe	Fail	Fail	Fail

Many lantern tests have been devised which have been used at different times or in different countries. The two main lanterns used in the UK are now described, with a brief mention of the standard lantern used in the USA.

Giles-Archer Lantern

The Giles-Archer lantern is used for routine investigation of signal recognition The standard lantern contains 6 colours: yellow, white, signal-green, green, red and dark red. Signal-green is the blue-green colour that is used as a standard signal colour. There is an aviation model with two additional colours, light green and signal yellow. The test is conducted in a darkened room. Before the test, the tester explains what will happen and tells the subject what colours will be used and what names should be used in response. However, the colours are not shown in advance, except for white and yellow. The colours are shown in a predetermined order with an exposure of 5 seconds each. At least 20 colours are shown, so that each colour is repeated several times. The lantern can be set to have either a 5 mm (large) aperture or 0.5 mm (small). The test is done first with the large aperture and only repeated with the small aperture if there is doubt about the results. The test is failed if there is a single error, classified as

- any misnaming of red

- any misnaming of green

- yellow called either red or green

- inability to see dark red at large aperture

Confusion between white and yellow, or the inability to see the dark red signal at small aperture, does not cause the subject to be failed.

Holmes-Wright Lantern

The Holmes-Wright lantern Type A is the standard test used by the armed services, the merchant navy and the Civil Aviation Authority. It is designed to test the ability to recognise standard coloured signal lights. British Standard BS1376:1974 sets out the internationally approved standards for signal lights. These were designed to recognise the problems of those with a colour vision deficiency, as far as that is possible. Thus green signal lights contain a proportion of blue to aid recognition. The test lantern contains two green lights, chosen to be at opposite ends of the range permitted by the standard, which are a yellow-green and a blue-green. One of the reds is a deep red corresponding to British Rail signal red. The lantern can show the lights at high or low brightness. Colours are shown in pairs and the subject is asked to name both. The 9 possible pairs are shown three times

Figure 28. **The Holmes-Wright lantern**

each, first at high brightness in a lit room, then at low brightness in a darkened room. The lantern provides a reliable and effective screening test. It has little diagnostic value; the number and type of errors made do not give a reliable guide to the nature of any colour vision defect.

A second version, known as the Type B, was designed for the Board of Trade to test colour vision of seamen. It is used in the United Kingdom and a number of other countries. Compared with the Type A Lantern, the coloured lights are dim and very small; they are intended to simulate distant navigation lights at sea. This makes the test difficult even for those with normal colour vision, some of whom may be expected to fail the test.

The Holmes Wright lantern is shown in Figure 28 with the front cover pulled out to show the cylinder that holds the coloured filters. The subject sees the coloured signals as a pair, one above the other.

Farnsworth lantern

The Farnsworth lantern, also known as the Falant, was developed for the US Navy. Compared with the Holmes-Wright lantern, the lights are larger and brighter, and the Farnsworth lantern test was designed to pass normal trichromats and those persons whose colour vision defect is mild. Approximately one third of those with mild colour vision deficiency are passed as suitable for naval duties. It is the standard test used in the USA for qualifying service and other personnel, being used by the US Coastguard, US Army and FAA examiners. In addition, it is used by some US railroad systems. Red, green and white lights are presented in pairs at different brightnesses, and the subject is required to name them. The red and green lights do not reproduce signal colours, but are chosen to represent colours that are likely to be confused by those with the more sever colour vision defects. The error score is the average number of errors made on three presentations of the nine colour pairs. A score of 1.5 or more is considered a failure.

Genetic testing

It is clear from the previous sections that there is no one satisfactory test that will provide a comprehensive and reliable diagnosis of the type and severity of a colour vision deficiency. A full diagnosis requires a battery of tests, using specialised equipment and an experienced operator. Most of the tests are unsuitable for use by young children. Additional problems are raised when there is a possibility that the subject is suffering from both acquired and congenital deficiency. On top of the problems inherent in the test, there is the possibility that the subject may be less than fully co-operative where a decision affecting livelihood is concerned. The attractions of a fully objective test are obvious.

The relation between genes and photopigments is now well established. Examination of the relevant genes contained in a person's DNA can both detect the presence of a congenital colour vision deficiency and diagnose its nature and severity. Such an examination can be carried out on a drop of blood and, should it be thought necessary, can thus be done on a child that is too young to undergo the normal test routine. At the present state of development, the genetic test is not a complete substitute for visual screening, as there are one or two ambiguities that need to be resolved with an Ishihara type test. Genetic testing should be able eventually to diagnose all congenital defects; development so far has concentrated on red-green deficiencies, since the relevant genes are situated near to each other on the X chromosome. For the immediate future, the most promising test for red-green colour vision deficiency would be a combination of visual and genetic testing. The visual screening test would be simple and suitable for use by young children. A follow-up genetic test would be used to confirm the visual test and provide information about the type and severity of any congenital red-green defect.

Test batteries

There is no one test that gives a complete evaluation and diagnosis of a person's colour vision deficiencies. Accordingly, a selection of tests is used that is appropriate to the

Table 13. **Tests used for evaluation of congenital colour deficiency**

Function	Scope	Tests
Screening	red-green defects	Ishihara plates
	blue defects	CU tritan plates
Screening & grading		Ishihara + CU tritan plates
		City University Test
		D15 test, Anomaloscope
Evaluation		D15, FM100
		Anomaloscope
Occupational screening	transport & armed services	Ishihara plates
		Holmes-Wright lantern

situation. Most people with a colour vision deficiency suffer from a congenital red-green deficiency and there is a series of well-developed tests to choose from. The rarer blue defects require a separate set of screening plates for their detection, since the Ishihara plates are not designed to detect blue deficiencies. Diagnosis and monitoring of acquired colour deficiencies are less well established and there are as yet no universally accepted standards. Those conducting measurements of acquired colour deficiency are likely to be actively involved in the research and development of testing methods.

Test procedures

The first experience of a colour vision test is likely to be a vision screening using a set of Ishihara plates. This may be done as part of a routine school medical or optician's eye test if the subject or their parent has expressed a suspicion of colour blindness. The tests are simple to use and administer and are very effective in detecting red-green deficiencies; a different set of plates is needed to detect the less common blue deficiencies. Notwithstanding the simplicity of the test, the tester should take care to administer it properly under correct lighting conditions.

There is no preparation required of the subject. It is not a test that can be prepared for and factors such as fatigue have negligible effect. Normal glasses or contact lenses should be worn; tests take place at viewing distances of 75 cm. Any loss of acuity caused by not wearing spectacles is unlikely to have a serious effect on the results of any test. However, the subject may feel uncomfortable and feel that a better performance could have been obtained if they had brought their glasses. Chapter 8 discusses the use of coloured lenses to improve colour vision. Tinted spectacles should not be worn. The tester should be aware of this possibility and ensure that the subject is not wearing a tinted contact lens.

A colour vision test can be confusing and disheartening to the subject. A person with colour vision deficiency, even a dichromat with complete absence of one set of photopigments, sees the world as coloured. It is likely that they realise that they have some form of colour vision deficiency, thought this is by no means always the case. However, it is most unlikely that they will be aware of the degree of the deficiency: they do not know how much they are missing. Most colour defectives probably think they are 'just a bit colour blind' and may be disappointed at the difficulty they experience in doing some of the tests. Inevitably, subjects will see the tests as some sort of examination, at which they want to succeed. The subject may feel that they would have passed the test - if they had tried harder - if the light had been a bit brighter - if the test display was closer or bigger, or if they could have looked at it for longer. This sense of frustration will be increased if the test is important for selection or continuation in an occupation. The tester must therefore be reassuring, show no disapproval or impatience, but ensure that the test is administered fairly. It would do no one a favour to pass a colour defective.

It can often be an advantage if the subject is accompanied. If a parent witnesses a child's examination, it will give them an important insight into the problems the child may have. The parent is able to see with their own (normal) eyes what the tests are like, and compare the child's responses with their own. Discussion with the tester will be of benefit in considering implications for future career prospects and life in general. An explanation of the way deficiencies are inherited is likely to be of interest to parents.

A full examination lasts up to one hour and will use a selection of different tests. The emphasis of the test will vary, depending on the age of the subject and the purpose of the test. The tester will start by recording some personal details and ask general questions about any known problems with seeing colours. There will also be some queries about situations or illnesses that could have given rise to acquired colour deficiency. The tester may ask about what, if any, difficulties are experienced at work or elsewhere. After the test, the results will be discussed with the subject. An experienced tester will have no difficulty in explaining the type of deficiency found. They will, however, normally exercise caution in making definite statements about the severity of the deficiency or the subject's suitability for employment. With the steady increase of legislation in all fields, any tester would wish to avoid making statements that might be challenged in court. A written report is normally provided where a full vision test is undertaken. This includes both the objective results of the tests, plus an opinion on the severity of the defect and the likely implications for employment. The use of a standard form saves time and ensures that no aspects are overlooked. A sample report on a subject's colour vision is reproduced at the end of the chapter.

The tester has to bear in mind that some subjects may want to cheat in the test. It may be important for the candidate to pass the test, to obtain or keep a job. There are many reports of would-be pilots in the Second World War attempting to pass the colour vision screening by more or less devious means. Learning the Ishihara plates by heart was effective for some. Using experience and intelligence to the full may improve scores on a lantern test; for instance naming any dim colours as red should improve scores for a red-blind subject. However, it would be virtually impossible to fake the results of an anomaloscope test. The opposite problem is the subject who wishes to fake a defect. This has occurred in connection with compensation claims after an industrial accident. Most of the tests in common use start with a demonstration. If the subject claims that the demonstration plate is unreadable, this may be an indication of malingering, as would be high and random error scores on the arrangement tests. It is of course possible for acquired and congenital colour defects to be present simultaneously; the tester must bear this in mind when faced with a set of apparently inconsistent test scores.

Personality tests

There are some so-called colour tests, which claim to evaluate personality from colour preferences. Strictly, they have no place in this chapter, since they do not diagnose colour vision deficiency. However they are often confused with vision tests and so will be given a brief mention. The American consultant Faber Birren, in his own words, *"vowed to devote his life to colour"*. He was an expert in the design of symbols and signage for factories, using strong shapes and colours to get the meaning across. He noticed that many people expressed strong likes or dislikes of some colours and that this seemed to relate to their personality type. He published a short book entitled *Character Analysis Through Color* in 1940, thus beating the better known Luscher test by several years. Both tests require the subject to select colours from a given range of samples and indicate liking or antipathy. The full Luscher test includes 43 selections from 73 colours, though a short version with 8 colours is more common. Luscher maintains that the result reveals personality and that the colours have an objective psychological significance. He even stated:

> *"Colour blindness makes no difference. The instinctive response to colour in terms of contrast makes the Luscher test valid even in cases of defective colour vision or even actual colour blindness, since the acceptability of some colour is somatically related to the degree to which anabolism and catabolism is needed by an organism"*.

This is indeed hard to believe. The fashion for the Luscher test has waned and one is unlikely to meet it now, whether in the consulting room or at a job interview. The colour deficient person should refuse to do it, though this risks another psychological diagnosis. This time it is Faber Birren speaking:

> *"If there be scepticism as to the whole idea of character analysis through colour, look for the possibility of emotional problems in the individual, Here loneliness and melancholia may be encountered"*.

Summary: Diagnosis

An examination of colour vision should provide information of the type of colour vision deficiency and its severity. No one test can provide all the information and it is necessary to use a range of tests to give a full diagnosis. The types of test in common use may be classified into the following categories.

Plate tests. The subject looks at a set of coloured printed plates and is asked to name the symbol that is hidden in a background of coloured dots. The most common example is the Ishihara test. This is a very effective test for detecting even mild red-green colour deficiencies. It does not detect blue or acquired deficiencies and gives no indication of the severity of the defect. The less common HRR test gives a measure of severity; the specialised City University tritan test is used to screen for blue defects, which may be congenital or acquired.

Arrangement tests. The subject is asked to arrange a number of coloured discs to form a steady progression of colour changes. The D15 test uses 15 discs and the FM100 test uses 85 discs presented in four separate subgroups. The D15 test allows a diagnosis of red or green colour deficiency. It is less stringent than the Ishihara in screening defectives. The pass classification includes mild colour defectives, who will have few or no problems in normal tasks. The FM100 test is a demanding test of colour discrimination and can be used to identify people with very good colour vision for occupations that demand it.

Anomaloscope. This test uses a piece of scientific equipment, wherein the subject looks in an eyepiece and sees two adjacent colour fields. One is yellow light, the other a mixture of red and green. The subject is asked to match the two halves by adjusting the proportion of red and green light, and the brightness of the yellow light. This test is useful for red-green deficiencies only. It gives the most accurate diagnosis and measurement of severity of the defect.

Lantern tests. The subject is shown a series of coloured signal lights and asked to name them. The test has little diagnostic value, but is used as a practical test for occupational purposes, particularly in transport or the uniformed services.

Genetic testing. It is now possible to identify the genes responsible for colour vision by direct measurement on a drop of the subject's blood. In conjunction with a simple plate test, this gives and accurate diagnosis and indication of the severity of a red-green defect. At present at the laboratory stage, the test is expected to become more widely available in future.

Sample test report

Colour Vision Clinic Report

Name: Mr D.A.McIntyre   **Date:** 02.02.96

The results of the colour vision examination show that Mr D.A.McIntyre has a colour vision defect known as protanopia. The defect is severe. Colour vision defects may be so slight as to be unimportant in everyday life or so severe as to cause a wide range of colour confusions. The following is a guide to this person's colour vision capabilities indicated by an x.

Colour recognition

1	Normal. The defect is of no practical significance	[ ]
2	Slightly impaired. Errors may occur with very pale colours or very dark colours	[ ]
3	Moderately impaired. Errors may occur with bright colours in some viewing conditions	[ ]
4	Poor. Gross errors occur in all viewing conditions	[X]

Sensitivity to Red Light

Normal [ ]   Defective [X]

Hue discrimination

The ability to distinguish small colour differences is

Average [ ]   Below average [ ]   Poor [X]

General Recommendations for Occupations involving colour judgements

1	Suitable for all types of work involving colour recognition except colour matching and colour quality control	[ ]
2	Suitable for most tasks involving colour recognition under good illumination and where speed is not important	[ ]
3	Suitable for tasks involving recognition of large colour differences only	[ ]
4	Not suitable for tasks requiring colour judgements`	[X]

Test completed

Ishihara Pseudoisochromatic plates	Fail. Red-Green defect
American Optical Company (H-R-R) plates	Fail. Severe protan defect
The City University Test (2nd edition)	Fail
The Farnsworth D15 test	Fail
Farnsworth-Munsell 100-Hue test	Protan axis of confusion error score 120
Holmes-Wright Lantern	In photopic viewing: Green called "White" White called "Green" Red called "Green" Green called "Red"
Giles-Archer lantern	In photopic viewing: Green called "Yellow" Yellow called "Green" White called "Green" Dark Red not seen
The Nagel Anomaloscope	Protanope

PART 2

The Effects of Colour Blindness

Chapter 5 - The appearance of colours

What does a colour-blind person see? Or, for that matter, what do normally sighted people see, and do they see the same colours as each other? Researchers in the laboratory can give good answers to questions about which colours look the same as each other, or which can be distinguished from each other. However, describing a sensation is altogether a different problem. In Isaac Newton's words, *"the rays are not coloured"*. We have seen in Chapter 2 how the eye analyses the wavelengths that constitute coloured incoming light. The eye sends a signal to the brain that tells the brain the proportions of red, green and blue in the light. The brain somehow processes this information to produce the sensation that we describe as colour. It is clear that the colour deficient do not see things in the same way as the colour normal. It is now becoming possible to produce colour transformations carried out by computer that can convey a good impression of the world view of the colour-blind. It is now possible to give a direct demonstration in answer to the old question *"what colours do you see?"*

Normal colour vision

Do all normally sighted people experience the same colour sensation? The answer seems to be that they do, more or less. Objective measurements show some variation between people in their ability to deal with fine gradations of colour. Some are better than others in making the fine colour discriminations required in colour arrangement tests and can produce more reproducible scores when using the anomaloscope to match yellow with a mix of red and green.

There is generally good agreement among people with normal colour vision as to what constitutes a pleasant or unpleasant colour combination, though this of course may change with fashion. This supports the view that colour sensation is shared between people. The relation between colours is of concern in the development of colour theories for artists. It is certainly true that some people are more sensitive to the subjective attributes of colours. For them, colour is important in their life and the choice of colour, whether for clothes or decoration, is of major importance. Colour is important in the visual arts and from time to time schools of art emerge in which colour is the major consideration, sometimes to the exclusion of form. However, there seems to be no evidence that those with "a good sense of colour" are in any way physically different from the rest of the normal population.

We may therefore confidently assume that there is a normal colour vision and that the sensation of colour is shared among colour normals. What, then, of the colour-blind? Remember, always, that the rather general term colour blindness covers conditions from the red or green-blind dichromats to those with weak anomalies, who have almost normal colour vision. In addition, there are the rarer form of blue defects and achromatopsia. Most of the discussion in this chapter refers to the common red-green forms of colour deficiency. Questions about what colours can be distinguished from each other can be answered precisely. The colour confusion lines in Figure 17 show just what colours are confused by dichromats. But this does not do much to convey to a colour normal what a colour defective experiences.

The first thing that must be realised is that, to a colour-blind person, the world looks normal and it looks coloured. Whether dichromat or anomalous, the colour-blind see the world as coloured, with no sense of anything lacking. Awareness of colour blindness only comes as a consequence of interaction with colour normals or with some aspect of the man-made environment. A child may hear adults enthusing about the autumn tints of the trees and wonder what all the fuss is about. Or they may be a bit slow in manipulating some colour coded apparatus at school. This may hold no significance to the child. The child is aware that people have a range of abilities, whether in catching a ball, drawing a picture or playing computer games. There would be no reason to suppose that seeing colours has a special category of its own. A surprisingly high proportion of colour deficient people reach adulthood without realising their condition.

The colour-blind person lives in a coloured world and it is a world in which people discuss colour and use colour names. The colour-blind learn to associate colour names with objects and usually manage to use them appropriately. Colour may be associated with a class of objects. Leaves are known to be green, and it is likely that leaves will be described, or indeed "seen" as green, even when they are actually brown or red. It may be that a colour name is associated with a particular object. A particular shirt may be known to be pink, even though it would look the same to its owner if it were actually a shade of blue or grey.

Give a dichromat a set of child's bricks, brightly painted in red, orange, yellow green and blue. There is little doubt that they will name the bricks correctly. How does this square with the fact that dichromats cannot distinguish between red, orange yellow and green? Chapter 1 explained how a colour can be described by its dimension of hue, saturation and lightness. The colour-blind will confound these dimensions and are likely to interpret changes in saturation or lightness as a change in hue. This is demonstrated by the attempts made to match yellow with a mix of red and green in the anomaloscope. Some results were shown in Figure 27. A red-blind subject can match yellow to red by reducing the brightness of the yellow until it appears the same colour as the red; to the red-blind, getting darker and getting redder are often the same thing. By using such cues as brightness, by relating appearance to known colours and by exploiting experience and context, the colour-blind adult will make more correct guesses than might be expected from their innate ability.

The size and brightness of a colour have a considerable effect on how it is perceived by a colour deficient person. A red object in a dull light may be difficult for a red-blind person to identify, yet be confidently described as red when viewed in sunlight. A red-blind person may happily identify holly berries as red when handling them, yet be completely unaware of their existence when looking at the holly bush from a distance. The reasons for these effects are not entirely clear. Possibly high illumination produces some response from the short wave cones which helps the eye to distinguish between red and green. A large image on the retina extends beyond the fovea, perhaps allowing some input from the rods. Whatever their cause, the effects of size and brightness are important. A person with a mild colour deficiency who can identify large, bright colours may feel resentful on 'failing' a colour vision test and argue that they could have passed if the light had been brighter. It often comes as a surprise to a colour defective that a normally sighted person can detect a coloured object by colour contrast alone, when the object may be too small to be seen as an identifiable shape. An example would be poppies in a field' of wheat; the colour defective has to see the shape of the flower before thinking about its colour. These effects of size and brightness emphasise the need for diagnostic tests to be carried out under standard conditions of illumination and viewing distance.

Using the strict term hue, rather than the more general term colour, it can be said that the dichromat sees only two hues. To them, objects are one of two hues, with varying degrees of saturation and lightness. In contrast, people with normal colour vision see more than 100 different hues. Dichromats confuse red with green, and they confuse with red and green all colours in the spectrum that fall between them, including yellow, orange and brown. They see blue and violet as the same hue, and the neutral point hue of blue-green is indistinguishable from grey. Now, it is fair to say that no dichromat would recognise themselves from this description; dichromats would say that they see many colours, but have difficulties with some shades. In fact dichromats become practised at using differences in saturation and lightness as cues and call these different "colours". The concept of a colour retaining the same hue while its saturation and lightness are varied is hard for a dichromat to grasp.

Understanding the world of the colour-blind is worthwhile for several reasons. It is important for the family of a colour-blind man to comprehend his limitations in selecting decorations and clothes, plus all the other every day activities discussed in the next chapter. It is even more important that parents have a sympathetic understanding of a colour-blind child's difficulties and are able to offer any necessary sympathy and support. Official bodies concerned with setting colour standards for safety critical signs need to consider the needs of the colour-blind. It is unfortunate that red and green became established in transport signalling so early on, before the problems of colour vision deficiency were fully appreciated. Awareness has taken a big step forward with the development of computers and the Internet. Commercial activity on the World Wide Web has led advertisers to consider carefully the legibility of their material. This, coupled with the ease with which computer programs can manipulate colours on the screen, has led to much interest in simulating the appearance of colours as seen by the deficient.

Simulation

Simulation of the visual world of the colour deficient to convey its appearance to the colour normal has a long history. As long ago as 1810 Goethe produced a water-colour landscape painting that was intended to demonstrate the view as seen by a blue-blind defective. Successful simulations became possible with the advent of the computer and colour monitor. It is now possible routinely to transform a coloured image in such a way that the transformed image will appear to a colour normal as the original does to a dichromat. Each coloured pixel on the colour monitor screen is defined mathematically by a set of colour co-ordinates. It is possible to write computer programs that will take each pixel and transform the colour to that seen by a colour defective person. These transformed pictures are very effective at conveying the reduced colour experience of the colour defective. They demonstrate that the colour-blind still see the world as coloured, but very much dulled down. They are invaluable in checking out colour contrasts and confusions when designing coloured images. The more thoughtful web page designers check out their designs to ensure that they are legible to all potential viewers. Unfortunately there is no way that any such transformation can be made in reverse. The colour-blind are not able to experience the world of the colour-normal, even for a moment.

How are these transformations made? In Chapter 3 on colour vision deficiency, Figure 17 showed sets of confusion lines in the chromaticity diagram. These lines show the groups of colours that look the same as each other to a dichromat. The basis of the transformation programs is that all colours in the original coloured picture that lie along one confusion line will be transformed to a single new colour. For example, if the transformation is being done to simulate the red-blind view of the world, colours lying along the confusion line that runs from red, through orange and yellow, to green, will be transformed to a single new colour. To be more precise, the chromaticity diagram determines the hue and saturation of the transformation, but does not show the lightness. The lightness of the transformation will be adjusted according to the sensitivity curve of the dichromatic viewer. For instance, while red and green are confused by the red-blind, red is seen as a dark colour. Thus, while red and green will be transformed to the same hue, the transformed red will be darker, to simulate its appearance to the red-blind.

This does not answer the question of which hue to choose for the transformation. In our example, all hues from red to green need to be transformed into a single hue, but which will represent their appearance as seen by a red-blind person? Objective experiments in the laboratory can tell us a great deal about colour discrimination and response, but they are not much use at conveying the sensation of colour. There has always been a philosophical dimension to considerations of colour: when two colour normals look at the same colour, do they experience the same sensation? There is little doubt that some people are more sensitive to colour; they have finer discrimination, remember colours better and care about colour more. However, it is unlikely that there are any fundamental differences in the way in which they perceive colours. The transformation problem is tricky. We require to choose a colour that gives the same sensation to a colour normal as the untransformed original colour gives to a colour defective.

A very few people are born with unilateral colour vision deficiency; they are colour-blind in one eye and colour normal in the other. This is very rare indeed and is not covered in the discussion on inheritance in Chapter 3. When unilateral colour vision deficiency is picked up in a test, the deficiency has normally been acquired through some illness or exposure to a chemical agent. Nevertheless, there are cases of true inherited unilateral colour deficiency. Such individuals are of great value to researchers, since they can compare the sensations experienced using each eye. It is therefore possible to say which colours look the same to a colour normal and to a dichromat. For red and green-blind persons, the invariant colours are a shade of blue and of yellow.

It is now possible to produce a set of rules so that any colour in the real world can be mapped on to a restricted set of colours as seen by a dichromat. Computer programs have been developed that will carry out this transformation for the three types of dichromat: red, green and blue-blind. There are now several versions of the software available. Further information on availability is given in the bibliography at the end of the book.

Simulating the appearance of colours for the weak form of defective colour vision, anomalous trichromatism, is more difficult. As was described in Chapter 3, there is a range of severity of the defect, so there is no single transformation that will do the job. The fact that the anomalous defective has three sets of colour receptors makes the computation of the transformation more difficult. It has been done, but involves analysing the image though a set of colour filters that each pass only a very narrow range of wavelengths. In this book, we shall concentrate on the dichromat transformations.

Colours on the Web

The explosive growth of the World Wide Web has led to a new profession of webmaster and a new approach to the design of coloured images. The freedom of colour choice available to web designers led to much poor design. In the early days, web pages intended to attract attention with the use of bright colours ended up hideous and illegible to colour normals and defectives alike. Designers began to pay attention to colour selection and to their credit, web page designers have taken the needs of the colour deficient seriously. There are several sources of information dealing with the art of designing pages that will be legible and attractive to the colour defective.

Coloured images used on the Web commonly used the so-called Websafe palette. By using a set of standard colours, designers can achieve a standard appearance for coloured images transmitted over the Web and viewed on a range of browsers and computers. Colours on a Web page are defined by a set of RGB colour values, each ranging from 0 to 255. This enables a total number of 256^3 colours to be defined. This number is in excess of 16 million, more than enough for the most colour sensitive, and bewildering for the designer. The web safe palette restricts the settings of each primary to the six values of 0, 51, 102, 153, 204 and 255, thus defining $6^3 = 216$ colours. The previous paragraph described how a computer can be used to simulate the appearance of an image seen by a dichromat. This possibility has been put to good use by web designers. **Figure 29** (see page 122) shows the Websafe palette plus its transformation as seen by a green-blind defective. Note how the defective palette divides itself into two halves, with blues to the bottom right and yellow-ochres to the top left. This reinforces the opinion mentioned earlier that dichromats see only two hues; the other colours they think they see are in reality changes in saturation and lightness.

Representations of the colour appearance of the Websafe palette as seen by the three types of dichromat have been produced by the BT research laboratory in the UK and elsewhere. The dichromat palettes may be loaded into a standard image manipulation application such as PaintShop or PhotoShop. It is then straightforward to copy the original image and transform the colours in the copy to give the appearance as seen by a dichromat. This is a valuable procedure for web designers working on sites where it may be critical that all users have good visibility. The transformation will quickly show up possible difficulties on the site, whether a confused colour coding or simple illegibility.

A selection of colours as seen by the three types of dichromat is shown in *Figure 30* (see page 123). This has selected some desaturated colours. A red-blind or green-blind person has great difficulty in distinguishing between these colours and would be hard pressed to name any of them. They would also find it difficult to remember the colours, say to identify a similar garment or carpet in a shop.

Images

The well-known map of the London Underground provides an excellent example of a familiar use of colour coding. Each of the lines has its own colour. The lines are identified in a legend but not named on the map itself. It illustrates the virtual impossibility of selecting a dozen or so key colours that will be readily distinguishable by dichromats. *Figure 31* (see pages 124-125) compares the view of the map seen by the three classes of dichromat. For red and green-blind, the Central and Bakerloo lines are indistinguishable from each other; the District Line is barely distinguishable from them. The Hammersmith and Waterloo lines form another pair that are hard to tell apart, with the Jubilee very similar, but a bit darker. The red-blind have a problem telling the Northern and Metropolitan lines apart; as always, the red-blind suffers the most problems of the red-green family of defectives. For the rare condition of blue-blindness, the Piccadilly Line appears dark green, perhaps dark enough to be confused with the Northern Line. These confusions create real problems for a defective unfamiliar with the layout of the Underground. The names of the lines are not labelled on the map and have to be identified by their colour. This can make planning a journey difficult. Fortunately, the platforms themselves are signed in words, so there is little danger of getting on the wrong train.

Figure 32 (see pages 126-127) illustrates the appearance of a fruit stall as seen by the three classes of dichromat. As was discussed in Chapter 6, selection of fruit is a real problem for the colour deficient. Changes of colour with ripening or spoiling mostly run along the red, orange yellow green axis, presenting the maximum difficulty to the red-green colour deficient.

Several software houses now offer transformation programs that will manipulate a coloured image to simulate its appearance as seen by a dichromat. **Figure 33** (see page 128) was taken from the web site of a firm offering such a package.

The simulation of the appearance of the visual world as seen by a colour defective cannot be perfect. Colour reproduction systems, whether on paper or on a colour monitor, are unable to reproduce the full range of colours available in the real world. There is also the problem of transforming the image from one medium to another. The colour reproductions in this book do not, and cannot, fully reproduce the colours seen on a computer monitor. For most situations of looking at coloured images the eye is fairly tolerant of the quality of reproduction. The phenomenon of colour constancy means that the eye-brain combination is good at seeing what it thinks ought to be the true colour, rather than what is actually there. As was mentioned in Chapter 2, the experiments of Edwin Land showed that the eye sees objects in their "true" colours, even when the standard of reproduction is poor.

As well as the difficulties of reproduction, there is the question of deciding which hues are seen the same by colour normals and defectives. The choice of blue and yellow is based on the experience of the rare individuals with one normal and one defective eye. It is of course difficult to argue that such an unusual individual represents the experience of the many colour deficient people in the world.

Subject to these cautions, the colour transformations illustrated in this chapter are very effective in providing a bridge of understanding between normal and colour defective. Certainly I, as a protanope, find the pairs of picture demonstrating the view of the normal and of the red-blind virtually indistinguishable. From the point of view of illustrating difficulties of colour discrimination, they are very effective. The illustration of fruit in trees shown in Figure 12 is a convincing demonstration of the problems faced by the early apes with two-colour vision.

For the colour normal, the pictures are enough by themselves to demonstrate the visual limitations of the colour defective. What of the colour-blind themselves? By themselves, the transformed pictures are of no great help. After all, the defective just sees two identical pictures, one labelled normal and the other labelled with their deficiency. Discussions with a sympathetic colour normal can be most illuminating - for both parties. The usual reaction when showing the simulations to a colour normal is one of surprise "*Is that really what you see!?*" followed by protestations of sympathy.

Summary: Colour appearance

It is now possible to transform a coloured image in such a way that its appearance to a colour normal is a good simulation of its appearance to a colour-blind person. The transformation is carried out using a computer program, several versions of which are commercially available. The programs carry out calculations that are based on two pieces of information. The first is knowledge of which colours are confused by colour defectives. The second is which colours produce the same colour sensation to a colour normal and to a defective. For red-blind or green-blind dichromats, the key colours are shades of yellow and blue.

The transformed images are very good at conveying to colour normals the restricted colour world of the dichromat. They can be invaluable to designers when producing coloured images that are required to be usable by colour blind people.

Chapter 6 - Everyday life

Colour vision deficiency profoundly affects the view of the world and so influences the interaction of the colour-blind person with the rest of the world and with other people. This extends over all sorts of activities: practical tasks such as choosing and preparing food, driving a car or repairing electrical appliances. It makes the job of selecting clothes more difficult and less enjoyable, especially since one of the reasons for choosing what one wears is to please or impress other people, who see things differently. Harder to deal with, because impossible to fully understand or quantify, is the sense of loss at the reduced enjoyment of colour, whether in the garden or art gallery. Poor colour vision may result in the deficient person being regarded as insensitive, because of their inability to judge another person's mood or health by skin colour. These are real disadvantages, suffered in varying degrees according to the type of colour vision deficiency. In many cases, however, the colour deficient person is almost, or even completely, unaware of the problem.

Problems with colour vision may surface unexpectedly. In 1986, Jeffrey Archer sued *The Star* newspaper for libel. Justice Sir Bernard Caulfield gave a notoriously biased summing up in the case. The judge had the court in laughter as he ridiculed a defence witness for his colour blindness and his inability to tell the colour of Archer's car. "*Aziz Kurtha has been a TV presenter. Not being able to recognise red, green or brown, he is hardly likely, is he, to be the presenter of Pot Black, or a commentator at the Crucible Theatre in Coventry (sic)? And if he did play snooker (if he could), you would not mind having a game with him, would you? And if you had a side-bet, would you not lay guineas to gooseberries you would win?*".

The relevance of colour vision deficiency to everyday life will be illustrated in this chapter, with the aim of providing some sort of bridge of understanding between the colour deficient and the colour normal. This is especially important in the case of a colour deficient child. The parents are more than likely to be colour normal and need to comprehend what difficulties their child is likely to face. The parents then will not make unreasonable demands and can help and guide their child to deal with such difficulties as may arise, whether at home or at school.

An important survey

The incidence of colour vision deficiency varies markedly across the world; this was described in Chapter 3. Western European populations, and countries with populations of European origin, have the highest incidence. Attitudes to colour vision deficiency vary across cultures. In Japanese society, colour vision deficiency is regarded as a defect and not normally admitted in public. A Japanese ophthalmologist describes how a colour-blind girl hesitates to get married; if she does she hesitates to have children. A mother who discovers her son is colour-blind is often distressed, since her father may never have revealed his deficiency. This is reflected in the higher number of careers that are barred to the colour deficient in Japan, compared with Europe. An organisation has now been founded in Japan to counter unnecessary discrimination. An international survey of attitudes would be of great interest. However, it has not yet been done and this section describes a study carried out in Australia.

While there has been much academic research into the details of colour blindness and its genetic inheritance, there has been surprisingly little on the experience of the colour-blind person. Where anecdotal experiences of the colour-blind have been reported, it is too often without any note of the type of defect suffered; a mild green-weak deficiency is far less of a problem than being red-blind. However, a study has been carried out in Australia that asked over 100 subjects with defective colour vision about their problems. This was a well-designed study, which took the precaution of asking the same questions to a similar number of people with normal colour vision to act as a control. Although the study was carried out in Sydney, there is little reason to doubt that the results are applicable to Western Europe or North America.

The subjects were selected from adult patients attending a clinic for an optometric consultation, not necessarily anything to do with colour vision. The questionnaire was administered in a consulting room, where confidentiality was assured and one could expect frank answers; this might not be the case if the subjects thought that their answers might influence their job prospects. Colour vision was tested, using the Ishihara plates as a screening test and following up with a full anomaloscope test to identify the type of defect. The subjects selected for the survey all had congenital red-green defects; those with acquired colour deficiency were excluded from the survey. The

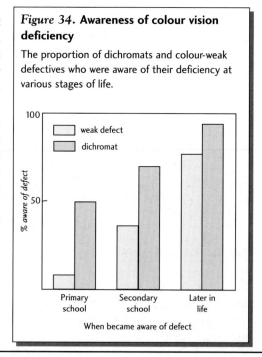

Figure 34. Awareness of colour vision deficiency

The proportion of dichromats and colour-weak defectives who were aware of their deficiency at various stages of life.

subjects were first asked if they knew that they had a colour vision defect. Only 5% of dichromats in the study, compared with 25% of the anomalous trichromats (i.e. red- or green-weak) were unaware of their deficiency. The age at which they became aware of having a colour vision deficiency is illustrated in **Figure 34**. This makes it clear that dichromats, i.e. those missing either the green or the red set of cones, were very much more aware than those with the weak form of defect. Many of the subjects with weak defects became aware of their conditions from a routine colour vision test, perhaps during a routine eye examination or on entry into the armed forces.

Table 14. **Percentage of subjects reporting difficulty with everyday tasks**

	P,D	PA,DA	Normal
Have you ever had any difficulty in selecting the colour of clothes, cars, paints, furniture, wallpaper or cosmetics?	86	66	0
With craft work and hobbies, do you have any trouble distinguishing the colours of wires, threads, wools, paints or other things?	68	23	0
Do you find plant or flower identification difficult?	57	18	0
Do you have difficulty in determining when fruit and vegetables are ripe by their colour?	41	22	0
Can you determine if meat is cooked by its colour?	35	17	0
Do you have difficulties because of colour as either a spectator or participant in sporting activities?	32	18	0
Do you find it difficult to adjust the colour balance on a TV satisfactorily?	27	18	2
Have you ever had difficulty in recognising skin conditions such as sunburn and rashes?	27	11	0
Have you ever taken the wrong tablets or medicine because of difficulties with colour?	0	3	0

How was it that any of these adults remained unaware of their deficiency until tested during the survey? When they were told, about half reacted with disbelief and an assertion that they were unaware of any difficulties they might have with colour. The rest, while surprised by the diagnosis, did acknowledge that they had some difficulties with colours. It is tempting to diagnose those who disbelieved the results as being in some form of psychological denial. Nevertheless, it is clear that the majority of children of primary school age who have a colour deficiency are unaware of it, and that goes for their parents and teachers as well.

The subjects were then asked a series of questions about difficulties they might experience in everyday life. The questions were used as prompts and the subjects were encourage to expand on their answers. The responses are summarised in **Table 14** (see page 99).

Dichromats (indicated as P and D in the table) reported difficulties more often than those with a weak form of colour vision deficiency (indicated as PA and DA). The survey found that those with a red deficiency reported more problems than those with a green deficiency; however, the difference was not statistically significant. Lack of significance does not mean that the difference does not exist, just that we cannot be sure from a survey of this size. From the nature of the disability, we would expect more problems with the red deficient type of colour blindness, and it may be that a larger survey would have produced a significant result.

The subjects were questioned about any problems they might have had while driving a car.

Table 15. **Percentage of subjects reporting difficulties with driving**

	P, D	PA, DA	Normal
Have you ever had difficulty distinguishing the colour of traffic light signals?	49	18	0
Do you ever confuse traffic lights with street lights?	33	31	2
Do you find brake lights on other cars difficult to see?	22	8	0
Do you find hazard or warning lights on temporary barricades difficult to see?	11	2	0
Do you find dashboard warning lights hard to see?	14	5	0
Do you find some road signs such as those on freeways or school crossings difficult to read?	5	11	0

Table 15 shows that nearly half of the dichromats surveyed report problems in seeing the colour of traffic lights. A more detailed breakdown showed that those with a red deficiency reported more problems that those with a green deficiency. It is also worth noting just how few colour normals report any problems. The question of whether colour

defectives have any greater risk of actually being involved in an accident will be considered further in Chapter 7.

Defective colour vision prevents the sufferer from entering some types of work and may present difficulties in any job. The subjects were asked if their colour vision deficiency had affected their choice of occupation and whether it created any problems in their present or previous occupations.

Table 16. Percentage of subjects reporting occupational difficulties

	P, D	PA, DA	Normal
Has your defective colour vision affected your choice of career?	43	29	NA
Have you ever been precluded from an occupation because of your defective colour vision?	24	23	NA
Do you have colour difficulties with your everyday work?	46	15	0
Have you had colour difficulties in any previous job?	24	22	0

Table 16 shows that colour vision deficiency has a profound effect on choice of career. Over one third of defectives have been influenced in career choice and one quarter have actually been turned down for the job of their choice. There is no difference in the figures between dichromats and those with a red-green weak type of defect. This is not surprising, since the Ishihara test does not differentiate between the two types, nor give any indication of the severity of the defect. Significant numbers reported difficulties in their present job. The survey went on to ask about the nature of the work and a surprisingly high number of the subjects with a colour defect were required to make some form of colour judgement at work. Perhaps this just reflects the ubiquity of colour coding in all jobs.

The survey shows that colour defectives do indeed experience a range of difficulties with a wide range of everyday tasks. As might be expected, dichromats, those completely missing one class of cones, have more problems than those with the weak form of colour deficiency. There were also indications that those deficient in red vision had more problems than those deficient in green; this is certainly so when the task involves the detection or recognition of red lights. Most people with a red-green weak defect found their colour deficiency more of a nuisance rather than a major handicap in everyday life. In this context it must be remembered that one quarter had been turned down for a job because of their vision. Dichromats reported more serious difficulties. As many as 86%

reported difficulties in selection of coloured goods, 68% experiencing difficulties in selection of materials for household repair and maintenance and 38% difficulties with foodstuffs. The survey gives a very good insight into the extent of the problems that people with a colour deficiency experience. We shall now consider in more detail what difficulties are found in different aspects of life.

Art

The word 'art' is almost synonymous with coloured images. An appreciation of 'fine art' is expected in the educated person. The rate of construction of art galleries in major cities, coupled with the enthusiastic attendances, demonstrates the widespread appeal. How does the colour deficient person appreciate art? What of the colour-blind artist? Most of this book is concerned with the objective practicalities of colour vision. Now we must bring in the emotional and subjective correlates of colour. The colour-deficient reader may have to be reminded that colour is very important, aesthetically and emotionally, to the normally sighted person; it's about more than being able to wire a plug correctly. Goethe took the artist's view of colour and found Newton's reductionist approach unappealing:

> Grey, dear friend, is all theory
> And green is the golden tree of life

There are artists for whom colour is all important, to the virtual exclusion of form or content. The approach may be intellectual, as with Josef Albers, who spent much of his life painting the series 'Homage to the Square'. The paintings consisted of nothing but nested squares in pure colours, squeezed straight from the tube. His concern was the way that the relationship between the colours affected the spatial relationship between the squares; art students are taught from the start about receding and advancing colours. Mark Rothko, on the other hand, painted giant murals of muted colours, whose object was to envelop the spectator and create a mood: so called colour field painting. The Rothko chapel in Texas is filled with murals described as virtual monochromes of darkly glowing browns, maroons, reds, and blacks; hardly designed to appeal to the red-blind.

Since the discovery of colour blindness, there has been speculation over the colour vision of artists in history. Some famous names have been discussed in this context: Uccello, Constable, Whistler. The discussions are inconclusive, lacking any corroborative evidence other than the paintings themselves. Artists who are known to be colour-blind seem to divide into two categories, those that play safe, using muted colours, and those that overcompensate, using bright colours that they feel confident with. Mondrian is said to belong to the latter category, using bright red, blue and yellow, while avoiding green. Leger is another. However, there is no independent evidence that either was actually colour deficient. Perhaps the most successful artist who was undisputedly colour-blind was Charles Nuttall. He had a successful career as cartoonist and illustrator, but is little known outside his native Australia. He was commissioned to paint a record of the opening of the first Australian Parliament in 1901. This vast oil painting, measuring twelve by eight feet, was executed in monochrome and contains four hundred individual portraits. It has been restored and now hangs in Museum Victoria in Melbourne. It is valued at over three million dollars, unquestionably a record for a colour-blind artist.

Patrick Trevor-Roper's *The World Through Blunted Sight* is a classic book on the relationship between painting and defective vision. The author was an ophthalmic surgeon with a wide ranging interest in art and in his book he describes a number of colour-blind artists. Among other things, he notes that an above-average proportion of engravers suffer from colour deficiency; he ponders whether they are failed artists, or whether a reduced ability to see colour gives them a superior skill in dealing with monochrome tones. Philippe Lanthony has described the work of the colour-blind engraver Charles Meryon, who produced a series of engraving of Paris in the middle of the nineteenth century. Many artists suffered from cataracts in later years. This has the effect of absorbing blue light, making the world appear reddish. Monet developed a double cataract and after 1905 he began to change the way he used colour in his paintings. Whites and greens became more yellowish, and blues more purple. He was persuaded to have a cataract operation in 1923, when he was well in his eighties. On his return home, he was reported to be surprised and distressed at the strange colours of his recent paintings.

Oliver Sacks, the American neurologist, maintains a lively interest in the vagaries of colour vision. Mention has already been made of his book *The Island of the Colour Blind*, which deals with a Pacific Island where a high level of consanguinity has led to a high proportion of people with achromatopsia. In another book, he describes the case of a painter who became completely colour-blind at the age of 65, following a relatively minor car accident. He suffered concussion and amnesia following the accident. He soon recovered, with his eyesight recovering full sharpness, except that he saw only in black, white and grey. The loss of colour vision occurred somewhere in the brain. As far as one could tell, the eyes worked perfectly well and sent the three colour signals to the brain, which failed to produce the sensation of colour. He viewed the world with a sense of distaste at its ugliness. He could hardly bear the changed appearance of people, his wife and himself included. Eating lost its pleasure, because of the greyish dead appearance of food. This form of colour blindness is so rare as to have little relevance to the types of colour vision deficiency with which this book is concerned. What is relevant to this chapter is the devastating sense of loss that the painter felt. The congenital colour-blind person of course feels no sense of loss, since they have never experienced a fully coloured world. Nor is the world of a dichromat as dull as the monochrome world of the unfortunate painter. The lesson to be drawn from the experience of the colour-blind painter is the importance of colour to those that can see it. This is at times difficult for the colour-blind to appreciate - perhaps when a partner insists on a particular choice of colour, or refuses some item of decoration or clothing.

Food

Over one third of colour deficient people in the Australian survey reported problems with foodstuffs, whether in buying or preparation. This is hardly surprising. According to evolutionary theory, the whole point of our developing trichromatic vision is to be able to find and select ripe fruit. This ability is severely compromised for those suffering from a red-green defect; as usual, dichromats are the worst off. Looking back to the chromaticity diagram, Figure 17 shows a line of confusion running along the right hand edge of the envelope for both red-blind and green-blind dichromats. That is, they see little difference in the range of colours running from red, though orange and yellow, to green. People with red or green weakness will suffer a similar confusion, though not to the same degree. This confusion coincides exactly with the colour changes undergone by many fruits as they ripen.

Shopping for fruit, especially now that self-service is almost universal, is a real problem. Of course, with practice, the colour deficient person learns a number of coping strategies. For many fruits, a squeeze will indicate approaching ripeness. But not always: it's too late if an apple feels soft to the touch. For a red-blind person, bananas are the most difficult, as the change from green to yellow is not accompanied by any change in lightness. I have occasionally asked for help from a fellow shopper, to be told that the yellow bananas are the ripe ones and the green ones aren't ready yet. Apples darken as they ripen and are not usually a problem. Pears, on the other hand, don't change colour much but do get softer. There may be more serious implications than ripeness. Under some conditions, potatoes develop a green tinge under the skin and to a lesser degree in the eyes; these patches are sometimes referred to as "sun-struck". The patches contain a high concentration of the alkaloid solanine, which is poisonous and of particular danger in pregnancy; solanine has been linked to miscarriage and spina bifida. Detection of the green tinge in potatoes is difficult for anyone with colour deficiency.

Meat changes colour, both before and after cooking. Within 30 minutes of exposure to air following slaughter, beef changes from purple to a bright cherry red colour. Over the next few days, the iron in the meat oxidises and the meat turns brown, indicating that the meat is no longer fresh. Here again, the colour deficient buyer finds difficulty in exercising judgement and usually plays safe by buying chilled or frozen meat from a supermarket. At the fishmongers, where freshness perhaps counts for even more than at the butchers, the standard advice is to look for bright red or pink gills on the fish; again, the colour deficient buyer is likely to play safe and buy frozen. For those that have the time and opportunity for old fashioned shopping, perhaps the best advice is to find a set of reliable family businesses and throw yourself on their mercy. The good ones know their business and are not likely to risk goodwill by knowingly selling off poor quality food.

Anyone attending a wine appreciation course will be told to use vision and smell in addition to taste when evaluating a wine. The colours of wines lie in the red-green part of the spectrum and so present difficulties to the colour-deficient drinker. The distinction between white, rose, and red wine, not to mention water, will present no problems. The range of colours within the red wine group is likely to be more subtle. Red wine oxidises with age and starts to go brown, giving an indication of the age of the wine to the experienced eye. This is what connoisseurs are doing when they tilt the glass; the change in colour is more clearly seen looking through the shallow edge, preferably against a white background. There is still a problem after the wine has been drunk and the bottle taken to be recycled. Separating green and brown bottles for correct disposal at the bottle bank is an impossible task for the person with colour vision deficiency. Reliance on the rule that wine bottles are green and beer bottles brown usually works, with the exception of some lager beers. One day I saw the notice "When the green bottle bank is full, use the brown one". It makes one wonder just how important it all is.

Sport

During the 1940s, boys' comics consisted of dense pages of small type. The *Adventure* comic ran a serial entitled *Baldy Hogan, Brains of the Team* that followed the fortunes of a football team that had a colour-blind goal keeper. To assist the keeper to distinguish between his own team and their opponents, Baldy added a large white roundel to the team's red shirts and socks. In practice, defective colour vision seems to have less effect on sports players than might be expected. Certainly, some team colours are hard for the colour defective player to distinguish, but there are usually sufficient additional cues to assist a player. Professional football players have their eyesight regularly checked and I am assured that the proportion of colour defectives is the same as that for the population at large. At high levels of play, players make decisions very rapidly, relying very much on peripheral vision. Outside the central area, the eye has poor colour perception but is extra sensitive to movement. It seems that colour vision plays little part in the performance of football players and I have failed to find any evidence of a problem.

However, the authors of *Coping with Colorblindness* tell a different story about Vinnie Testaverde, a well-known player who played quarterback in an American football team. Every now and then he would throw a long pass straight to a member of the other side. It was soon realised that he was colour-blind. Action was taken to ensure that opposing teams wore contrasting uniforms and this resolved the problem.

For sports and games that do not require instant reactions or decisions, there is time for the colour defective player to consider the situation or ask for help. The brown snooker ball can certainly give problems. However, the experienced player will normally be able to distinguish it by slight shade differences; if there is a problem it is always possible to ask for help. Peter Ebdon achieved international status without his defective colour vision proving a significant handicap. Red and green buoys are used to mark the course in yacht racing and the colour defective helmsman has problems in detecting and identifying them. In practice, the handicap should not prove too severe. A plan of the course is available in advance, with the red and green buoys marked; the helmsman needs to memorise or note the course to ensure that he will know which way to go round each of the markers. Nevertheless, the single-handed sailor with defective colour vision is at a disadvantage; the buoys are less visible and decisions have often to be made quickly in the stress of racing conditions, with little time to consult any notes.

Gardening

One day at the garden centre, I reached the checkout carrying a potted rosemary bush. The checkout operator looked a bit embarrassed: "Excuse me, but that plant is dead". Indeed it was: dead brown and live green leaves were indistinguishable to me. Usually the colour deficient person can tell the difference between life and death in the garden by the flexibility and feel of leaves and twigs. In general, working in the garden is not difficult for the colour-blind person. Flowers and berries will take longer to find and often have to be identified by shape rather than by colour. Pick-your-own raspberries and strawberries do not present a problem, but the rate of picking is likely to be slow. Ripening of these fruits produces steady darkening and it is easy to distinguish between ripe and unripe. As was discussed in the section on evolution, a background of dappled leaves in sunlight makes finding objects difficult. Shapes are broken up and the main cue for colour normals is hue. This is true not only for flowers and berries, but for orange secateurs and other tools, which are too easily lost in the garden by the colour deficient. Power tools designed for garden use are supplied with orange cable. This is intended to contrast visibly against a background of grass, to reduce the chance of accidental tripping or cutting through a live conductor with a lawnmower. However, for a red-blind gardener, the cable is a pretty good match for healthy grass. The message, as always, is to be aware of the problem and take a bit of extra care.

Perhaps more important than the practical difficulties mentioned is the loss of full enjoyment of the colours of flowers and the relationship between them. The colour deficient gardener is more likely to concentrate on shapes and shade contrast than on colour harmony. However, fashions change, and the grey and white garden is the height of sophistication in some circles.

Dress

Ask someone if they were aware of any friends or colleagues who were colour blind, and the answer is often "Oh yes, I remember him; he wore those strange clothes". Choice of clothes is the most obvious public expression of colour preference and needs to be taken seriously by the colour deficient person. Expressing one's personality through clothing is fine, but needs to be under control. The deficient person runs the risk of making unusual or bizarre selections and remaining unaware of the effect they produce. We start from the premise that dress selection is important. If not, why are so many shops and magazines, and so much expenditure, devoted to it. It is perhaps difficult for the colour deficient person to comprehend how important a good or bad colour selection of clothing may be in some situations.

The colour deficient person may be hard put even to name a colour that they like and usually has little or no concept of whether a colour suits them. It's worth discussing with a friend or partner what are the best colours to wear and then working within this colour range. For most clothes that are available in a range of colours, the label carries the colour name. Labels are not a great deal of help when buying clothes. Manufacturers adopt the same free and easy approach to colour naming as do paint manufacturers. The label should help in deciding whether a shirt is pink or blue, and the often difficult distinction between navy blue and black. However, the more creative names are of little help. A quick browse through a catalogue produced ivy, taupe, stone, boulder, driftwood, basil; names that convey little.

There is little substitute for advice when buying. The shop assistant should be able to prevent the worst mistakes, but only if the buyer has some idea of what they actually want. The assistant can help you avoid buying a pink shirt by mistake, but only if you know you do not want a pink shirt. Selecting what tie to wear with what shirt should only be a problem the first time round. Advice from a sympathetic friend or partner should produce a number of safe selections, which the colour-blind wearer can then stick to. The wife of the former Conservative party leader, William Hague, is reported to pin labels to his clothes when he travels without her. It is possible to learn what goes with what, even if one's own judgement is no guide. Many colour deficient people adopt the strategy of grouping their wardrobe into 'brown' and 'blue' categories and selecting an outfit from garments within a category. There is no excuse for wearing mismatched socks; few socks of different colour happen to be identical in material, weave, length, pattern and all the other cues that serve to differentiate them.

When John Dalton was honoured with a doctorate from Oxford University in 1836, he appeared at the ceremony wearing a crimson coloured cape. He had commissioned this from a tailor, after selecting the material himself. His Quaker faith deprecated the wearing of loud colours and Dalton stated honestly that the cape appeared black to him. However, given his awareness of his defect, it is hard to say at this distance of time whether Dalton had made an honest error or was making a public demonstration of his colour blindness.

The problems with dress extend to the more subtle, but perhaps more important, personal coloration. The person with colour deficient vision is insensitive to skin, hair and eye colour. One anecdote tells of a young man who had lost a number of girl friends because he complimented them on their lovely green complexions. However, if this story is true, the man must have been singularly unintelligent as well as colour-blind. One soon learns what colour names are associated with objects or situations; the phrase "she turned green" is associated with sea-sickness, not beauty. The red-blind person is quite unable to experience the problem of "red-eye" in photographs. The vascular retina at the back of the eyeball is illuminated by a camera flash and gives the person in the photograph the appearance of having red pupils. Nevertheless, the colour deficient photographer is quite aware of the problem, since it is mentioned in every photo manual, and will take appropriate steps to avoid it. New developments in digital photography and associated image processing software give both professional and amateur photographer enormous freedom to control colours in the final image. This is a mixed blessing for the colour deficient. The software programs will give a precise reading of a coloured pixel in colour co-ordinates. This makes it possible to match colours exactly when editing, but the ability to modify colours is daunting for the colour defective.

It is in the region of subtle shades that the colour deficient person has great difficulties. The range of flesh tones means little, and a colour deficient person may appear to be insensitive in their inability to detect blushing, pallor or ill health. The range of expressions, such as white as a ghost, blue lips, turning green, in the pink of health, red as a beetroot, green at the gills, may be familiar to the colour-blind as phrases, but have little meaning as far as appearance goes. Sunburn is likely to be felt before the colour change in the skin is noticed. As with so many other things, the colour deficient person must use their head rather than their eyes in taking action, in this case applying a sun block in time to prevent any skin damage.

These things matter, whether in a marriage or other important relationship such as parent and child. The colour deficient father or husband is going to have difficulties in noticing changes in complexion, whether due to make up, mood or illness. He can make the effort to compensate by paying more attention to other cues, but the compensation will only be partial. On the other hand, parental reaction to a teenager dying their hair red is likely to be muted, or even non-existent.

Decoration

Many of the observations that were made about choice of dress apply equally to the choice of decorations for the home, except that decoration is more expensive and more permanent. Perhaps the hardest thing for the colour-blind partner to accept is that the choice of colours in a decoration scheme is actually important and matters to the other partner. Why spend £1000 on a new carpet that looks exactly the same as the old one? The answer that it doesn't go with the new curtains hardly seems an adequate reason. The usual situation is of course a colour deficient husband and normal wife. There are reported cases of depressed women who only cheered up when their husband died and they could redecorate the house. This seems an extreme reaction to a minor problem. The more typical situation would be the husband grumbling about the trouble and expense of redecorating, which for him produces little gain. This should be resolved within the normal ambit of relationships. The colour deficient home decorator of course has problems and will need help selecting materials. Overpainting one colour may be a problem if they appear similar; it is only too easy to leave the old colour grinning through the new.

If left to themselves, people with a colour deficiency seem to go for dull colours, relying on contrasts of texture, light and shade to provide the interest. Why they should go for dull colours is unclear, since one might expect that they would compensate with over-bright colours. However, this doesn't seem to happen.

Children

The ability to see and distinguish colours develops very early in the human infant. By the use of various research techniques, such as measuring electrical impulses from the brain (EEG) or by using psychological techniques to investigate responses, it is possible to investigate responses to colour long before the child is able to speak. It has been established that colour discrimination is almost up to adult standards by the age of two months. Reasonable ability in naming and matching colours is developed at two years, with increased accuracy at the age of four.

At school

Being able to name colours has always been regarded as a marker in a child's development. The modern primary school environment is rich in colour, with much of the equipment and decoration in bright colours. Colour coding is used for many descriptive purposes and the use of colour as an aid to teaching appears in many forms. The Cuisenaire system was widely used during the 1960s for teaching number concept in primary schools. The system involved the use of rods whose length corresponded to a number value. Each length of rod had its own colour, which the teacher used as a name to refer to the rod. The physical representation of number value was held to assist in teaching children to grasp number relationships. For instance, there could be a practical demonstration of the different combinations of rods that added up to the same total length. Certainly colour deficient children suffered greater confusion than normals in handling the rods. An acquaintance remembers that as a boy he could not master Cuisenaire mathematics because he could not pick out the rods when they were referred to by colour name. The school was unhelpful, even when his colour problem was pointed out, and only removal to another school put his education back on track. There have been various reading schemes in which coloured text is used to indicate the sound, e.g. the *ough* in bough and the *ow* in cow would share the same colour, but be different from the colour of *ough* in rough. One scheme used 40 different shades. While these schemes present obvious difficulties for colour deficient children, there seems to be no evidence that they suffer educationally in the long run. Infant teachers seldom report cases of difficulty. Rather surprisingly, there seems to have been little research into the effect of colour vision deficiency on the schoolchild. However, what research has been done shows that the child is unlikely to suffer any educational handicap. One statistical study found no relationship between colour deficient vision and elementary school achievement.

Testing children for colour vision used to be a routine part of the school health service. Screening was done at around the age of eleven years. This has now largely been discontinued, partly on the grounds that there was little consistency in what was done with the results of the screening. It was also the case that some of the screening was carried out to a poor standard. It was pointed out in Chapter 4 that the Ishihara tests must be administered under controlled conditions to obtain reliable results. The parents, class teacher or careers teacher might be informed of the result and the pupil given a leaflet on the nature of colour blindness. At present in the United Kingdom there is no consistent policy on testing. There seems to be no good reason why testing should not be universal and carried out while the child is at primary school. Colour vision deficiency is not a serious disability and no special provision in teaching is required. However, there are frequent occasions when the child may experience difficulties and a sensitive awareness on the part of the teacher can serve to mitigate them. A child may be bewildered by colour references but find it difficult to explain what the problem is, or be reluctant to do so. At least the modern whiteboards have eliminated the use of coloured chalk on a green board. It is unfortunately true that there is little awareness of colour vision deficiency by teachers and it is not treated as part of teacher training. In contrast to the British attitude, the Japanese Ministry of Education required the Japan Textbook Publishers Association to set up a committee to review textbooks for ease of use by colour-blind students. The result was the publication in 1986 of *Guidelines for Color Prints Used in Textboooks to Help Color Defective Students*. The recommendations have resulted in better colour combinations in Japanese school textbooks.

There are too many anecdotes of unsympathetic handling of colour-blind children by uncaring teachers, who seem to be unaware of the difficulties it may cause. It is possible that the colour-blind child may be regarded as a nuisance, and of course they may become a nuisance in order to divert attention from the problems they are experiencing. This story comes from the USA, from someone who was only diagnosed as colour-blind in his twenties, when he attempted to train as a pilot. When he was in a primary class, the class was given a routine colour vision test:

> The very bored and tired looking lady asked me to read out the number or letter on each page. Well, I simply could not do it, I told her there was no letter or number. The lady looked at the clock on the wall, grew very angry with me and told me that she knew I was a trouble maker in class, and look again. I was very scared by this time, and the last thing I wanted to do was get in trouble again, as it was almost a weekly ritual with me at this point in my life. So I tried very hard, but I could not see any numbers or letters, except on maybe 2 or 3 of the 15 pages. The lady grew very frustrated and angry with me, berated me even more and said "Look again here, there's the letter B, can't you see it?" While by this time I was fighting back tears on the inside, so I said yes, anything to get the hell out of that room and avoid trouble. The same coaching happened on a couple more pages and then I was dismissed back to my classroom. Shortly later school ended and I ran home, too terrified to tell my parent about this event.

Colour is used widely in the primary school, to provide contrast, create interest and provide a stimulating environment. Colour is used extensively as a means of classification. Cuisenaire rods and reading schemes are particular examples, but colour is used in sorting games or as a simple shorthand description; look in your green book. Generally, colour-blind children are reluctant to admit or broadcast their problem and will develop coping strategies. They will probably learn to recognise the particular green book, or even the green in that series of books, but will not recognise another shade of green as belonging to the same class of colours. An experienced teacher, who has a colour-blind son, has given advice. A child may be colour-blind if they:

- choose a colour and constantly call it by a different name

- are unable to thread beads from a model, or only though constant trial and error using direct comparison

- are unable to continue a colour pattern

- are unable to follow instructions with colour as a key element, but are able to follow instructions of similar difficulty when colour is not present.

She also gives some practical advice on coping with colour-blind children in the classroom:

- be aware that the use of colour is not a skill that can be taken for granted and that inability to distinguish colours can hamper learning

- be aware that colour has only a limited place in some children's lives

- use symbols instead of colours for many purposes

- to assist children in art activities, use colours consistently. Lay out the colour palette the same way each time and teach the child the order of the colours

- remember that it is possible, though less likely, for a girl to have a colour vision deficiency.

At secondary school level, the problems are more specific. Some areas of practical science demand precise colour judgement. Traditional test tube chemistry requires judgement of colours in chemical analysis. Measurement of the strength of chemical solutions is done by the method of titration, where one chemical reagent is dripped into another until the colour of an indicator changes. Litmus is the oldest and best known chemical indicator, but there are many others. Colour judgements are required in crystallography when using a polarising microscope and there are many examples in biology where colour judgement is important. Coloured charts and maps are always a problem, where there may be a legend of 10 or so colours to differentiate between different areas. Viewing a diagram through a red filter can be a great help in this situation; this will immediately differentiate between reds and greens. The colour deficient student learns to cope with most of these problems, by a combination of experience and co-operation from friends. It is a problem though and especially so in exams. If problems or difficulties are anticipated, the student should always approach the teacher in advance of the exam. Most examination boards will take into account a statement of the problem submitted by the school.

At home

In the nature of things, most children with a colour vision deficiency have normal parents, who may have little insight into the difficulties faced by their child. The mother may remember that her father was colour-blind, but only recall that he didn't talk much about it. Moreover, as was shown in the Australian survey, many children and their parents are unaware even of the existence of a colour vision deficiency. This can produce problems for the child and, at its worst, lead the parents to become irritated at the apparent slowness or unwillingness of the child to do some tasks. As always, a bit of knowledge and understanding are of great help. If colour vision deficiency is suspected in a child, whether because of confusion with colour names or in distinguishing coloured objects, or because of a family history, it is worth arranging for a colour vision test. This is not, it must be emphasised, to label the child as "defective", but simply to assist the parents in realising where some difficulties might arise.

If a child has difficulty in naming or distinguishing colours, the instinctive reaction is to spend some more time in teaching them their colours. This is perhaps not so silly as it sounds. No amount of training can improve colour vision. However, hardly anyone is completely colour-blind and it is as well to reinforce the grasp of the colours that the child can see. The parents can reinforce the association of colour names with objects, such as green grass and red pillar boxes. This gives useful points of reference and may save the child from using inappropriate colour names. It is possible to learn specific colours. For instance, the local buses may be coloured red or green. When seeing an isolated bus for the first time in isolation, the child with a colour vision deficiency may not be able to decide with any confidence what colour it is. However, the two colours are unlikely at appear identical. If the two colours are seen together, and the child is told which is which, they will be able to remember appearance and identify them in future. Of course, this may not help in another town where different shades of red and green are used.

Summary: everyday life

Poor colour vision creates problems in many areas of life. Surprisingly, many colour-blind people, even those dichromats who are lacking either the red or green photopigment, are unaware of the extent of their deficiency. Difficulties in selecting colours of clothes or decorations are commonplace, as are problems in judging ripeness or quality of foodstuffs. People with poor colour vision are very poor at appreciating changes in skin colour, whether from sunburn, illness or blushing. They may be problems at school, especially in primary classes where difficulties in dealing with colour coded education material may be interpreted as backwardness. For parents the most important thing is simply to develop an awareness of difficulties that the child may have, to provide unobtrusive assistance when required and avoid putting the child into situations where it will be confused or risk failure. Do remember that people with a colour vision deficiency do see the world in colour and do not dismiss their observations.

Chapter 7 - Careers

Many jobs exclude colour-blind applicants and for many young people who are unaware of the nature of their deficiency the exclusion comes as a shock. There are many other jobs that have no formal colour vision requirements, but where poor colour vision is a handicap to effective working. It is surprising that such problems were not recognised until the nineteenth century. Most work in the pre-industrial age was related to agriculture, where the inability to judge ripeness or quality of fruit and vegetables must have been a real disadvantage. Presumably, colour defectives were regarded simply as poor workers and relegated to ploughing or ditch digging.

It was the growth of shipping and rail transport in the nineteenth century that brought the question of colour vision at work into prominence. Coloured lanterns were introduced for signalling. At sea the meanings of green for starboard and red for port are fundamental, remembered by generations of cadets by *port wine is red*. The colours are used for port and starboard navigation lights on moving ships and as coloured buoys to mark the right and left boundaries of navigable channels. For land transport, first for trains and then for motor vehicles, the basic signals are red for stop and green for go. On both land and sea, the same unfortunate choice of colours that would be confused by the colour deficient was made from the start. The early days of the railways were marred by some major accidents. Probably most were caused by operational demands running ahead of the limits of contemporary technology, but many were caused by human error where apparently a signal was not seen, or not acted on appropriately.

The medical officer of the Paris - Lyons Railroad was testing employees for red-blindness as early as 1855, apparently in advance of any serious accidents having been attributed to this cause. Two railway accidents in the nineteenth century were attributed to defective colour vision and they led to the widespread introduction of screening for colour vision deficiency. An accident at Arsley Junction in England was blamed on a colour-blind driver failing to see a red stop signal. There was much speculation in contemporary newspapers as to the cause of the accident. Since both driver and fireman were killed, it was impossible to be sure about this, especially as other evidence suggested that the signal in question had frozen up in the cold weather. Nevertheless, the widespread concern led to the introduction of a maritime colour vision standard by the Board of Trade during the following year.

In 1875 there was a major accident in Sweden when a train driver apparently failed to respond either to a green (which then meant caution) or to a red light, and failed to stop. The resulting crash caused 9 deaths, including all those implicated in the accident. The crash was taken to confirm earlier concerns about the safety of colour deficient staff and the Swedish railway authorities commissioned the development of a colour screening test. The result was the Holmgren wool test. This test involved matching a large number of samples of dyed wool. Although the test continues in limited use to this day, it is time consuming and not always reliable. A screening test using a coloured signal lantern is directly relevant to the problem and was introduced in 1891.

The safety record at sea seems to have been worse than that on the railways. Many accidents during the last century were ascribed to faulty colour vision. In separate incidents during 1869, a ship confused its position in the English Channel and went aground. In both cases, flashing red and white lights on navigation beacons were misread. An English captain confused the end of Marseilles pier with a reef by being unable to differentiate between red and green signal lights and went aground. There were many more such cases.

Even when the importance of colour vision began to be recognised, there were problems with enforcement. In some cases, masters who were known to be colour deficient, and who had already caused accidents, were allowed to continue at sea. If they owned the vessel it seems there was no one to stop them. Colour vision testing was in its infancy and not reliable. As the law stood in Britain, a seaman who succeeded in passing a retest was allowed back to sea, even in cases where he admitted he could not tell the difference between green and white lights. Perhaps in some cases, the ability to recover colour vision was genuine. Acquired colour vision deficiency due to excessive tobacco smoking was not uncommon among seamen; certainly the loss of a steamer off the coast of Florida was ascribed to this cause.

Career groups

For most occupations, colour deficiency produces the same minor problems as in everyday life. These difficulties can be overcome with a bit of care and common sense, plus, when required, a little bit of help. However, for some occupations colour vision is important. It is helpful to classify these into groups.

Group 1. In this group of occupations, the ability to see and respond to colour coded information may be critical to safety, with potentially fatal consequences if a signal is misunderstood. This group includes the transport industry and most uniformed services. Normal colour vision is a formal requirement for entry.

Group 2. Occupations that involve working with coloured materials and where the consequences of error may be expensive, though without safety implications. Employers may give a colour aptitude test, but often do not.

Group 3. Occupations that are not primarily to do with colour, but where some tasks involve identification of colour, such as indicator colour changes in analytical chemistry. There is rarely any consideration of colour vision in entry qualifications or selection of candidates.

This classification ignores the self employed, who generally make their own rules. There are successful colour-blind artists, garden designers and architects - all fields where deficient colour vision would seem to impose a severe handicap. However, with sufficient talent, and enough self awareness to concentrate on strengths and avoid areas where the deficiency would be a problem, successful careers can be achieved. Some occupations require sensitive colour judgement over a limited part of the colour space and it may be that colour deficiency is no handicap. The grading of diamonds, where mistakes are indeed expensive, requires colour judgements along the blue-yellow axis. A red-green colour defective may perform perfectly well in this task.

Table 17 is reproduced from a leaflet widely circulated among schools careers officers. Some of the occupations will be considered in more detail in the rest of the chapter. The list is not necessarily complete and some of the categories that require good colour vision offer an alternative test to the Ishihara plates, which would allow those with a mild colour deficiency to qualify. If the matter is important to you, check the entry qualifications directly with the appropriate regulatory body.

Table 17. **Classification of occupations**	
Occupations where defective colour vision may be a problem	
Armed Forces	Check requirements with the Armed Forces Career Offices
Civil Aviation	All flying personnel (airline transport pilot, flight engineer, radio officer), air traffic controller, private pilots and most engineering apprentices
Electronic and electrical engineering	
Fire service	Normal red-green vision required
Motor mechanic	
Police	
Railway	Staff on operating duties or working amongst moving traffic, or doing electrical or safety-critical work

Table 17. Classification of occupations (continued)

Occupations where defective colour vision may be a problem

Artistic work	Graphic design, picture restoration
Beautician	
Buyer	Textiles, yarns, foodstuffs, etc.
Cartography	
Engineering	Some categories
Florist, horticulture	
Interior design	
Colour matching	Textiles, paper, ceramics, paints, dyeing
Pharmacy	
Carpet weaver, inspector	
Colour photography, TV	

Medicine

John Dalton, the chemist who first described colour vision deficiency, noted that blood looked a *"bottle-green colour"*. This would suggest that doctors and others in the medical professions may experience difficulties if they suffer from defective colour vision. The problems are more wide ranging than the recognition of blood. Illnesses can produce changes in skin colour that are very difficult to detect or evaluate for someone with poor colour vision. There are also many specific examination or diagnostic techniques that depend on colour change. This seems fairly obvious, yet the difficulties faced by doctors with poor colour vision have received little attention, even within the profession.

The situation was made clearer by a survey carried out in the UK a few years ago. Forty doctors with congenital red-green colour vision deficiency were recruited for the study; they were given a full colour vision test battery and asked to complete a questionnaire on their experience. They were mostly GPs and all were aware that they had a problem, though they did not necessarily know the precise type or severity of the deficiency. Over half the sample reported problems in their professional practice. The most common involved:

- widespread body colour changes, such as pallor, cyanosis (blue lips and fingers), jaundice (skin yellowing)

- rashes and erythema of the skin

- reading charts, slides, prints and codes

- evaluating test strips for blood and urine

- ophthalmoscopy (examination of the retina)

- detection of blood in bile, urine, faeces or vomit

- examination of the ear

About the same number recalled having difficulties while at medical school. Rather under half the sample reported no, or at least very few, difficulties. Some of those reporting no problems were diagnosed as severely colour deficient. This raises the question that they may have been unaware of their failings. There have also been some studies of the performance of doctors with a colour deficiency under test situations when carrying out specialist tasks, such as the identification under the microscope of diseased tissue samples. The worse the colour vision deficiency, the poorer the performance was found to be.

There are general problems in diagnosis. A good doctor uses all relevant experience when presented with an ill patient and this includes general appearance. Changes in skin colour, whether sun tan, blushing, jaundice or a hot flush, are very difficult for the colour deficient doctor to evaluate, or even detect. Pallor, 'turning green' or blue lips may all pass unnoticed. Skin rashes are not at all obvious. Other problems are more specific. A red-deficient doctor or ophthalmologist will have great difficulty in making retinal examinations through an ophthalmoscope. The first sign of a life-threatening melanoma is a small area of black melanin pigment in the retina, which the colour deficient will have difficulty in distinguishing from a small haemorrhage. The presence of blood in vomit or faeces is easily missed by a colour deficient nurse or doctor.

The practice of medicine is becoming more and more dependant on the use of electronic instrumentation for diagnosis and treatment. This is of great benefit to the colour deficient practitioner, since reading a digital display presents no possibility of error. This helps the anaesthetist, who has traditionally used skin colour as an important indicator of the state of the unconscious patient. Behind the scenes in the pathology lab, diagnostics tests are carried out on blood, tissue or other samples. Examination of tissue samples depends on staining sections and then examining them under the microscope for diagnostic or identification purposes. The colour defective will work under difficulties, related to the degree of deficiency. There are several colorimetric tests used in the medical laboratory, where the amount of colour change in a reagent indicates a measure of the quantity tested. A well known one is that used in the monitoring of diabetes. A stick coated with the chemical reagent is dipped into a urine sample and the resultant colour compared with a printed chart to measure the concentration of sugar. Colour deficient medical staff may have a problem with this test. The disease of diabetes can induce a blue/yellow colour deficiency, which makes it difficult for the patient when carrying out a self-test. Electronic instruments, which analyse a drop of blood and provide a digital readout, obviate the problem.

The proportion of doctors with a colour vision deficiency is the same as that in the rest of the population, which means that in the UK there are about 6000 colour deficient doctors, of whom 2000 are general practitioners. While poor colour vision undoubtedly produces difficulties in diagnosis, it is rare that a colour observation is the crucial sign. Those aware of their deficiency take greater care, and colour-blind doctors are considered by themselves and by others to perform as well as other doctors with normal colour vision. However, the problems are real. One doctor who failed to detect blood in vomit commented *"the patient was lucky to survive"*. It is certainly a matter of concern that a good proportion of doctors with a colour vision deficiency are unaware of the fact; those who are aware of their limitations are more likely to take extra care.

Problems have been reported in dentistry, not with the quality of repair work, but in colour matching crowns and other prosthetic work. The new cap has to be matched carefully to the colour of existing teeth, which can cover a range of colours in the unsaturated yellows and browns - just those that a red-green colour defective finds hard to distinguish. When plastic capping materials were introduced, there was apparently a surge of legal actions in the USA by patients complaining that their new teeth did not match the old. This was attributed to poor colour vision among some dentists; the problem is resolved by computerised colour matching or by advice from a person with normal vision.

Only one medical school in the UK screens applicants for colour vision. Very few do so in the rest of the world, though Taiwan screens all medical students. There is a strong case for giving all medical students a colour vision test. This would not exclude the colour deficient from a career in medicine. However, it would help a student understand any limitation and assist their choosing a specialist career within medicine that would be compatible with the severity of any colour vision deficiency. The situation is similar for veterinary science. At least one school requires students to make the staff aware of any colour vision deficiency, so that appropriate advice and assistance can be given to the student.

Figure 24. The Farnsworth-Munsell FM100 arrangement test

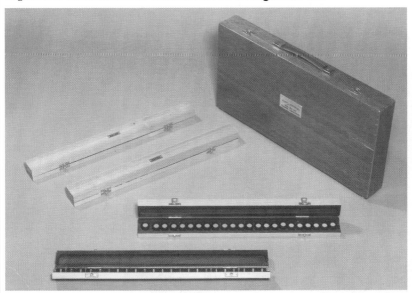

Figure 26. The Nagel anomaloscope

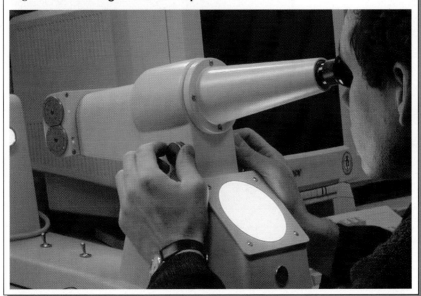

Figure 29. Websafe palette

The Websafe palette of 216 colours and as seen by a green-blind viewer (Visibone).

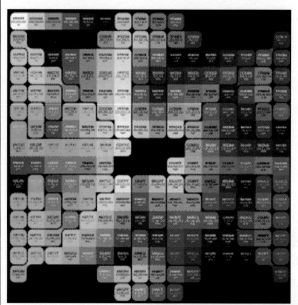

Figure 30. Websafe selection

The 27 normal colours have been produced by all combinations of 0, 50 and 100% levels of red, green and blue primaries. They have then been transformed to show their appearance to colour-blind viewers.

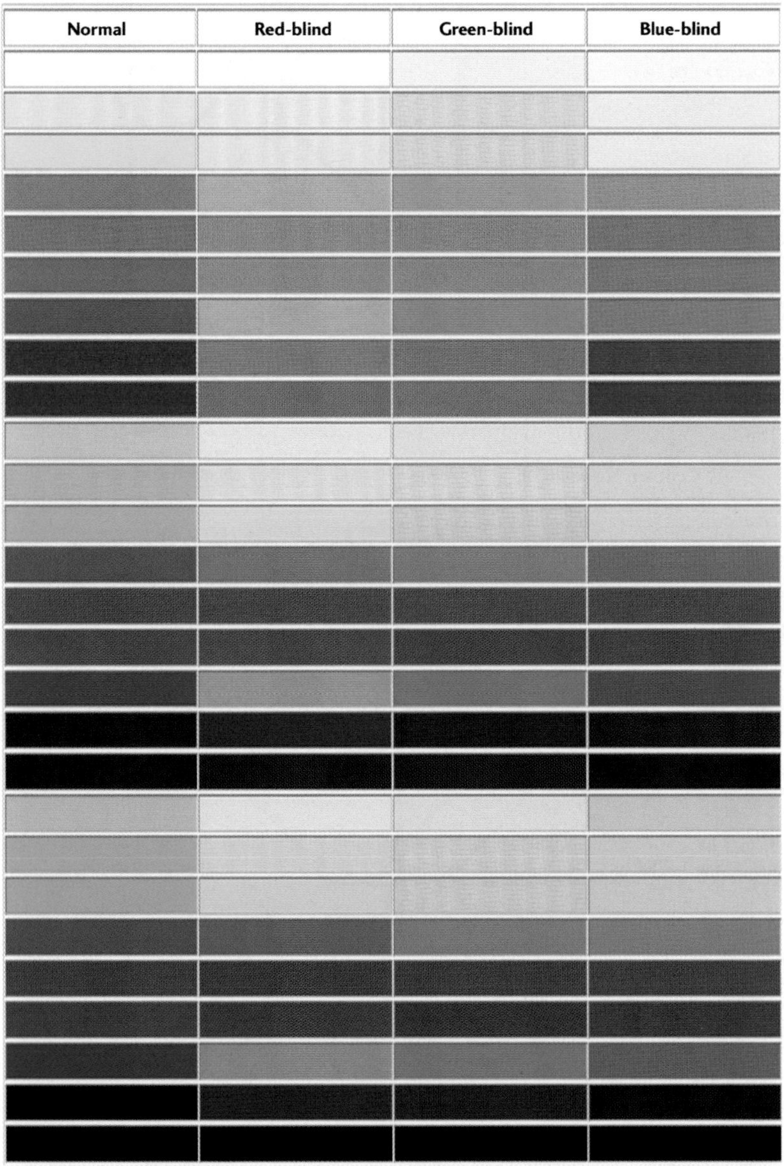

Normal	Red-blind	Green-blind	Blue-blind

Figure 31.
London Underground

Part of the London Underground map, as seen by colour normal (A), red-blind (B), green-blind (C) and blue-blind (D).

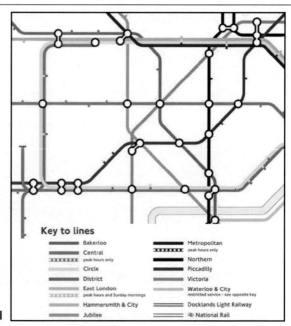

A. Colour Normal

B. Red-blind

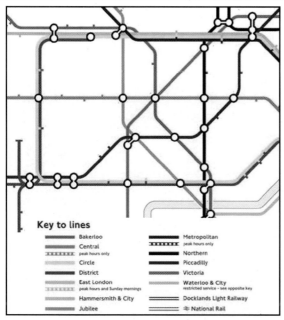

Key to lines

Bakerloo	Metropolitan
Central	peak hours only
peak hours only	Northern
Circle	Piccadilly
District	Victoria
East London	Waterloo & City
peak hours and Sunday mornings	restricted service – see opposite key
Hammersmith & City	Docklands Light Railway
Jubilee	⊀ National Rail

C. Green-blind

D. Blue-blind

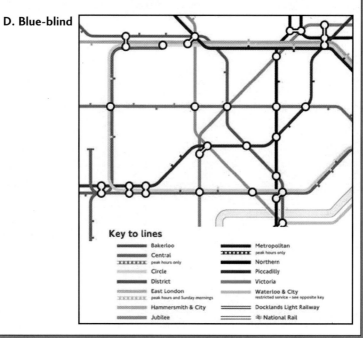

Key to lines

Bakerloo	Metropolitan
Central	peak hours only
peak hours only	Northern
Circle	Piccadilly
District	Victoria
East London	Waterloo & City
peak hours and Sunday mornings	restricted service – see opposite key
Hammersmith & City	Docklands Light Railway
Jubilee	⊀ National Rail

Figure 32. **Fruit stall**

A fruit stall as seen by colour normal (A), red-blind (B), green-blind (C) and blue-blind (D) shoppers.

A. Colour Normal

B. Red-blind

C. Green-blind

D. Blue-blind

Figure 33. Transformations

The normal image (A) has been transformed using Colorfield ™ Insight software to simulate the appearance to red-blind (B), green-blind (C) and blue-blind (D) users of the Web.

A. Colour Normal

B. Red-blind

C. Green-blind

D. Blue-blind

Horticulture and agriculture

There is a strong case to argue that human colour vision evolved to enable us to find ripe fruit in the trees. For colour deficient people, the problem nowadays is selecting the fruit at the greengrocers, rather than finding it up a tree. The colour changes gone through by a wide range of fruit and vegetables during the ripening stage cause particular difficulties to red-green defectives. The colour change is typically green, through yellow to red, and this lies along the confusion lines for red-green defectives. Examples are bananas, lemons, oranges, dates, melons, tomatoes and much soft fruit.

Normal colour vision is therefore helpful for anyone working with plants, whether in agriculture, horticulture or market gardening. Since instant, life or death decisions are not called for in these occupations, it will be possible for a colour deficient worker who knows their limitation to cope satisfactorily. A worker who is unaware of the problem or who is unable or declines to ask for help may make expensive mistakes. A problem was experienced by a market gardener in Dorset, whose major crop was tomatoes. Some staff were picking fruit that was either immature or else overlooking it when ripe and allowing it to spoil on the plant. Either way, the fruit was useless. Not only that, but extra time was wasted in sorting and rejecting the poor quality fruit. The employer was advised to screen future employees for colour vision. Magenta filters were provided to help the colour defective tomato pickers to select fruit of the correct ripeness for picking. The problems extend beyond growing and picking, to sorting and grading. Modern supermarkets prefer to present fruit and vegetables that are evenly matched in each box. Indeed, it is now an EU regulation that perishable foods must be packed in groups that have reached a similar stage of ripeness.

As with so many things, the nature of the disadvantage will depend both on the colour task and the type and severity of the colour deficiency. Where the colour task is well defined, i.e. the same sort of colour judgement has to be made repeatedly, it may be possible to use tinted spectacles as an aid. It is an unfortunate fact that a tinted filter that improves discrimination between two colours that might otherwise be confused, will produce a confusion between some other colours. Where the task is repetitive, such as telling green tomatoes from red tomatoes, a filter may well improve performance. The selection and grading of tobacco leaves is an activity of great economic importance and mistakes can be financially disastrous to a company. The importance of good colour vision has been recognised by the industry and most employers require normal colour vision as assessed by the Ishihara colour test. Workers with a very mild defect, or normals who would like further help, may find their performance assisted by viewing the leaf through a magenta filter.

Textile industries

The modern textile industry employs a very wide range of dyes and pigments and applies these to an ever increasing number of synthetic and natural materials. Above average judgement of colour is required both in the production of coloured yarns and fabrics and their incorporation into fabrics, garments and carpets. The industry relies more and more on objective measurement of colour, using spectrophotometers and computer matching techniques. These are especially useful for the control of automatic processes. However, the final judgement remains the human eye, since it is the eye of the ultimate customer that has to be satisfied.

The normal eye is extraordinarily sensitive to small differences in colour and can easily detect when two colours do not quite match each other. This presents difficulties to clothing companies that commission garments from different sources. It is not uncommon in a dress shop to find a top made in Europe that is partnered with a skirt made in Asia; the difficulties in ensuring a perfect match are great, and not always overcome. Colour matching of fabrics is made more difficult if the two fabrics are not themselves the same. The fibre, weight of cloth and the texture of the weave will all affect the colour appearance and give rise to apparent differences, even if the colours are identical.

Carpet weaving requires the operative to set up a loom with the required coloured yarns. The bobbin boy who sets up the loom may be required to place up to 10,000 bobbins of up to 32 different hues on a single loom. The bobbin boy works alone and the working practice is often such that the selection is not checked by anyone else before starting the production run. Clearly, a mistake made at this stage will result in the production of a considerable length of faulty carpet, at great financial cost. Finished carpets are inspected and minor faults corrected by hand. The requirement for good colour vision continues down the line, through warehousing and despatch, to the retail operation. Surprisingly, in laboratory tests on the ability to detect small, but commercially unacceptable, differences in colour between cloth samples, colour defectives proved as able as, if not better than, colour normals. The colour defectives were able to discriminate small differences, but could not name the colours. Presumably, the faults involved a difference in saturation or brightness, rather than hue alone. While a colour defective may prove satisfactory at detecting faults, they should certainly not be relied on to provide an accurate match.

There is no central authority advising on colour vision requirements. For jobs where good colour vision is important, larger companies often screen applicants, using the

Ishihara plates and sometimes the FM100 Hue test. This is certainly to be recommended; the Ishihara plates should be supplemented by the City University tritan test to ensure that any blue defectives are detected. Following a number of expensive errors caused by poor colour judgement, some textile companies decided that a more sensitive test than the Ishihara was required when screening staff for critical jobs. Their solution was to develop a variation of the FM100 hue test, but to use a selection of coloured yarns that had proved problematic in practice. Four different shades of black and a very dark green had proved particularly difficult for some operatives to distinguish and were included in the test. It is sometimes reported that colour defectives have an ability to detect differences that are invisible to normals. This may be so in particular situations, but is not to be relied on. It would be inadvisable for anyone who knows or suspects they have colour vision deficiency to enter the textile industry, unless it is for a job not primarily concerned with colour.

Transport

Coloured lights and signals are in general use over the world in all forms of transport, whether by land, sea or air. It was the occurrence of some serious accidents at sea and in the new railways during the nineteenth century that led to the imposition of colour vision tests for train drivers and seafarers. Those with a colour vision deficiency are unarguably at a disadvantage in the detection and interpretation of coloured signals. Few would disagree with the requirement that professional drivers and pilots pass a colour vision test. However, car driving is a near universal activity and a necessary part of participating in much of modern life. Is the problem of colour deficiency serious enough to call for restriction or banning of colour defectives and if so, from what activities? How important are individual rights, including the rights of the disabled to participate fully in life? To what extent should the relevant authorities be required to provide signals that are usable by the colour deficient?

Colour is used to convey information in two ways. One is to give instructions and information that require action; the other is to improve visual displays and make their information more readily understandable. Traffic lights are the obvious example of the first; the colour coding of traffic and direction signs an example of the latter. Colour signalling is used in all forms of transport. Coloured signal lights are the most effective method available for a visual signal that has to convey information over a long distance. A signalling code that relied on shapes or letters would not be legible over the same distance. A red light at night can be seen very much further than a sign saying "Stop".

Generally, transport colour signals employ up to five colours. Red and green are the most important, with white, yellow (amber) and blue added where more colours are needed. While there are often additional cues that may help the colour deficient in interpreting the signal, e.g. the position of traffic lights, this is not always so. Navigational lights seen at night at sea, or a coloured flare fired from a control tower offer no clues other than colour as to their meaning.

Colour is also used to help organise a display and to help the viewer to recognise the signal. Here, the colour does not carry the message itself but assists the user to find it. Traffic signs in Europe have a well-organised classification that uses both colour and shape to indicate the type of message. Red circles are prohibitive (e.g. no overtaking), blue circles give positive instructions (e.g. ahead only) and signs in a red triangle convey a warning (e.g. slippery road). Direction signs use a green background for main routes and white backgrounds for local routes; motorways are picked out in blue. The colours and shapes are well chosen and assist even the colour deficient in rapidly finding the required information. This can be most important, given the large amount of information that may be displayed at a complex road junction.

There is no doubt from laboratory studies that colour defectives have problems with coloured signal lights. These are:

- an increased reaction time to the lights. Red-blind observers are the slowest in responding to a coloured signal, with a reaction time up to twice normal, i.e. up to half a second.

- an increased number of errors in identifying colours. Errors are most frequent with red, yellow, green and white. Unfortunately, it is impossible to select a three-colour code that can be reliably recognised by all colour defectives. However, as long as the signals are reasonably large and bright, red, green and blue signals can be distinguished by all except the red-blind.

- a reduced visual range. Red-deficient observers have to be closer to a red signal to see it. Both laboratory and field studies show that red-deficient observers have to be twice as close to a red stop light to recognise it.

However, these findings in themselves are not enough to justify a ban on all colour defectives from all transportation activities. The activities need to be considered separately.

Driving

"What about traffic lights?" is probably the most common question asked of a colour-blind person. In practice, it's not much of a problem. Traffic lights in most countries are positioned vertically one above the other, with STOP at the top and GO at the bottom. The colours have been chosen to be as clearly differentiated as possible for a range of colour deficiencies. There are however problems, which may not be obvious to the colour deficient drivers themselves. Traffic lights are often seen against a multi-coloured background of shop display lights and the defective driver is likely to take longer to notice the set of lights. Once the set of lights has been seen and identified, it is not a problem to decide which one is switched on. The red-deficient driver finds the red light dimmer than the others. The red in traffic lights and that used in red brake lights contain yellow or orange, and so are reasonably visible to the red-blind driver. The colour is quite different from the dark red signal used in the lantern test, which is almost invisible to the red-blind observer. The reduced visibility of a red traffic light is most likely to be a problem in bright sunlight, where it my be difficult to tell if it is illuminated. The situation is worse if the light is viewed against a rising or setting sun. Problems with identification may arise if the lights are of non-standard colour, which the driver has not yet learnt, or are arranged in an unusual pattern. In Holland, there are some traffic lights associated with level crossings where the green signal light is above the red, a potentially highly dangerous situation. Another example is the lights over the entrance to the Mersey Tunnel in Liverpool, marking the tidal flow traffic lanes. The red and green lights are of non-standard colour and arranged side by side. This makes it difficult for the colour defective driver to make what may be a rapid decision as to whether a lane is open. But, as always, there are ways to cope. The defective driver either follows the car in front or sticks to the left hand lane. It would, of course, have been better if the traffic engineers had reinforced the coloured signals with a red cross and a green arrow.

It would seem simple enough to check whether colour deficient drivers do in fact have more accidents than their normal counterparts, but this has proved surprisingly difficult to demonstrate conclusively. Epidemiological surveys are always bedevilled with the problem of ensuring proper sampling and avoiding the confounding of different factors. We can be quite sure that colour defective drivers have more accidents than drivers with normal vision; this is because most colour defective drivers are male, and males drive more miles and drive less safely than women. Amazingly, some surveys on accident rates and driving have not recorded the sex of the drivers. Setting the inadequate surveys aside, the scientific literature reports many studies, between them analysing accident statistics of thousands of drivers in several countries. The surveys fail to find any significant difference between the accident rates of colour normals and defectives. All surveys, that is, except one. A careful analysis was made of 2000 drivers who had been involved in accidents in the Dresden area of East Germany during the mid 1970s. It was found that red-deficient drivers had twice the number of rear end collisions as normals, especially under conditions of reduced visibility or in conditions when braking distances are increased. This is consistent with the laboratory observation that reaction time for the response to coloured signals is increased for the red deficient. However, there was no difference between overall accident rates for defectives and normals.

The position, therefore, is that colour defectives have some problems with driving, but this is not reflected in a higher accident rate. The World Health Organisation recommended in 1956 that no driving restrictions should be placed on the colour deficient and this is the situation most countries. The United Kingdom has no colour vision requirement for a car or Large Goods Vehicle (LGV) or Passenger Carrying Vehicle (PCV). Some authors have recommended that colour defectives should not be allowed to become professional drivers; some suggest only the red-deficient should be banned. It is open for employers to insist on normal colour vision in their drivers. For example, the policy on colour deficient drivers of passenger carrying vehicles varies between local authorities in the UK. A driver may have had a trouble free career with one authority, but find it impossible to make a transfer elsewhere.

Aviation

International agreements require pilots of commercial aircraft to have normal colour vision. In countries where private flying is more common, criteria for obtaining a pilot's licence are often less restrictive. In the USA, applicants who have normal colour vision, or who have defective colour vision but pass the Farnsworth lantern test, are classed as colour-safe and granted an unrestricted licence. Applicants who fail the lantern test have the right to be given a supplementary test, which consists of recognising the colours of a control tower signal gun. The test passes most mild red-green defectives, 30% of green-blind and 20% of red-blind. Those passing the test are granted a waiver. In this way, about half of those normally classed as colour deficient may obtain a pilot's licence.

In the United Kingdom, the Civil Aviation Authority (CAA) oversees the licensing of pilots. UK medical standards were harmonised with European regulations to produce the Joint Aviation Regulations (JAR), which came into force in 1999. Two classes of medical certificate may be issued: Class 1, which covers all commercial flying, and Class 2, which covers all private flying. The CAA uses three classifications for colour vision. These overlap with the classification used in the Armed Forces and are summarised in Table 18.

The classification is based on performance on the Ishihara plates and Holmes-Wright lantern tests.

Table 18. Colour vision classification

Grade	Terminology		Test criterion	
	CAA	UK Armed Forces	Ishihara	Lantern
CP1	-	exceptional	pass	pass at low luminance
CP2	normal	normal	pass	pass
CP3	safe	slight deficiency	fail	pass
CP4	unsafe	severe deficiency	fail	fail

The CAA colour vision assessment starts with the Ishihara test. For CP2 classification, the applicant must make no errors. A candidate who fails the Ishihara test is then assessed with the Holmes-Wright lantern; the procedure is described in Chapter 4. The prospective pilot is allowed three runs of the lantern test, each with 9 presentations of coloured lights to be named; this part of the test is carried out in a normally lit room. If after the first run of 9 presentations, no errors are made, the applicant is classed CP3 and no further testing is done. If there are any errors after the first run, two further runs are carried out in the same lighting conditions. If these are performed without error, the applicant is classed as CP3. If either of the two further runs contains errors, the subject is allowed to become dark adapted and a further run is carried out in darkroom conditions. If no errors are made on this final run, the applicant is classed CP3. However, if errors still occur, the subject is classified as CP4 (unsafe). If any errors are made at any stage during the test naming green as red or red as green, the classification is CP4 with no further testing.

Both CP2 and CP3 are considered satisfactory for a Class 1 medical certificate. Applicants who are classed CP4 can be issued with a restricted Class 2 certificate, which allows them to fly in daylight under Visual Flight Rules. Thus it is now possible for a severely colour-blind person to obtain a private pilot's licence and also become an instructor of private pilots, albeit with some restrictions on use. A mildly colour-blind person who is capable of passing the lantern test can obtain a Class 1 medical certificate and go on to fly commercial aircraft.

Surveys of flying accidents in the USA have shown that colour deficient pilots, in this case those with a waiver, have substantially more accidents than the colour safe; the colour safe group itself includes some mild colour defectives. However, it turns out that pilots with defective colour vision had much greater flying time, presumably because those seeking the waiver had a greater need or desire to fly than the average pilot. When this is taken into account, the difference between the groups disappears into the statistical noise. There was, however, no attempt to see if the type of accident was related to any failure to respond properly to coloured signals.

Until recently, the situation in Australia was similar to that in the USA, and it was possible for a colour defective to obtain a restricted licence that bars the holder from night flying. The reasoning behind this is that the identification of coloured signal lights, whether ground based or aircraft navigation lights, is more critical at night when there is no visible object to help identify the situation. This ruling was challenged by a green-blind Australian, who was a medical practitioner as well as an enthusiastic pilot. He challenged the ban on night flying in the courts, a campaign that was to last for 20 years. Under Australian law, it was possible to take the case to an Administrative Appeals Tribunal, which is empowered to review regulatory matters. The existing rules were strongly defended by the Australian Department of Aviation. The court heard evidence from academic researchers as well as practising pilots. After 40 days, the court rejected the proposition that defective colour vision posed any threat to the safety of air navigation. The consequence was that the ban on night flying was lifted and colour-blind people are free to obtain a pilot's licence in Australia. Some restrictions were imposed. There was no right to fly in the airspace of other countries without express permission. In addition, those with red deficiencies had to demonstrate that they could detect the presence of a red signal light, though not necessarily know what colour it was.

Some countries still maintain severe restriction on pilots with colour vision deficiency. Given the changes in legislation in Australia, we may expect this to be questioned. There is a strong demand for the rules to be changed. During the Australian hearings, the legal challenge was supported by over 1000 colour defective pilots. Modern aircraft have highly sophisticated instrumentation and an increasing amount of information is presented via video displays - the so-called glass cockpit. Situations where visual identification of red or green signals is safety critical are becoming more and more infrequent. Information is passed to the pilot by radio rather than by signal light and computers monitor the performance of the aircraft. On the other hand, the presentation of information on video screens is often itself highly colour coded. While it is still legible to a viewer with a colour deficiency, the speed of interpretation is inevitably slowed.

Maritime

The amateur sailor is remarkably free of regulation. While anyone with any sense would get training first, there is no qualification or test that is required by the UK authorities before taking a boat to out to sea. The colour deficient skipper is at a serious disadvantage when spotting and recognising coloured navigation lights. In practice, the instinct for self preservation seems to operate reasonably well and colour deficient amateur sailors learn to work within their limitations. Modern electronic navigation equipment gets ever cheaper and can accurately determine a boat's position to within a few yards using satellite technology.

The situation is controlled for professional seafarers. The Maritime and Coastguard Agency publishes the medical and eyesight standards for seafarers. Deck officers and ratings are tested with the Ishihara plates. Those who fail may request a retest using a Holmes-Wright lantern. Engineers and radio operators also require good colour vision; in this case those who fail the Ishihara plate may ask to be retested using the Farnsworth D15 or the City University Colour Vision test. No specific standard is prescribed for other categories of seafarer, other than that their colour vision should be adequate to allow them to undertake their duties. Those passing the whole medical are assessed as fit for unrestricted sea service. Anyone in charge of a local passenger vessel requires a boatmaster's licence. A doctor is required to certify that there is no "evidence of a colour vision defect likely to lead to inability to distinguish red, green and white lights at 1 mile distance". The wording implies that an Ishihara test is acceptable, but does not state a pass-fail criterion. Surprisingly, the form specifically prohibits wearing the X-Chrom contact lens by name, but does not mention other tinted lenses. The use of tinted lenses as an aid for defective colour vision is discussed fully in Chapter 8.

Railways

Railway organisations were among the first to recognise that defective colour vision presented a safety hazard. Signalling with coloured lights is still an essential part of the railway system and strict standards are laid down for employees. As far as possible, the conditions are specific to the job function, so that colour defectives are not barred from jobs that have no safety implications. There are four job classifications, each with its own set of regulations:

- Train drivers. All train drivers are required to have normal colour vision.

- Train workers. This category includes all those dealing with the movement of trains, e.g. platform workers, shunters &c. All workers in this category are given a colour test and graded. Normal colour vision is required for specified jobs, such as shunter. A platform guard is not required to have normal colour vision, since the responsibility for safe operation rests with the driver.

- Signallers. All signallers and crossing keepers are required to have normal colour vision.

- Track workers. All track workers are given the Ishihara test and graded. Normal colour vision is required for specific functions, such as lookout, foreman or signal installer.

Armed Services

By and large, the colour vision requirements for the armed forces follow those described in this chapter for similar civilian occupations. Colour vision requirements are enforced for the obvious categories, such as pilot or electronics technician, but colour vision deficiency is not an overall bar to service. Certainly, colour blindness never excused anybody from National Service.

It is widely believed that colour-blind personnel were recruited by the armed forces to spot enemy camouflage. There is good scientific reason to believe that this could have been the case. Chapter 1 showed that all colours in real life are made up of a mixture of several colours of different wavelengths. A sodium street light is about the only monochromatic source of a single colour to be found outside the laboratory. Two coloured objects that appear identical may be reflecting a different mix of colours, which are seen as the same by the normal eye. A camouflage paint that has been mixed to match, say, the background colour of leaves may not in fact reflect the same underlying wavelengths as do the real leaves. A colour defective observer is unlikely to see the two colours as the same. This is equivalent to the Hidden Digit plates in the Ishihara colour vision test. With these plates the colour defective sees a number, whereas the normal viewer sees only random dots. It should therefore be easier for a colour deficient observer to spot camouflaged objects where the camouflage is based on matching colours.

There is another camouflage principle where the colour deficient observer may have an advantage. An important function of camouflage is to break up recognisable outlines, using irregular patches of drab colour, usually greens and browns. A colour defective observer is generally less sensitive to colour information and is more likely to see the solid shape underlying the misleading coloured patches. This ability has been demonstrated in the laboratory. However, in spite of the potential advantages, there seems to be no definite evidence that colour deficient observers were ever used in warfare to detect enemy camouflage.

Camouflage is widespread in nature, and has developed to make prey harder to detect by their predators. Many colour defective hunters in the USA consider that they have an advantage over their colour normal colleagues and claim they are often the first to spot their quarry. Professor Mollon has speculated that in human evolutionary history, there may have been an advantage for a hunting group to maintain within itself a sub-group with specialised skills. Colour defectives would have been useful members of the hunting party and this may have helped the survival of their genes.

Electronics and telecommunication

Electronic components, such as resistors and capacitors, have for a long time had their values identified by a colour code. Each device is identified with a number of coloured rings giving the value of the device based on a code containing 12 colours. This is well beyond the capacity of most colour defectives to deal with. However, the image of the electronics technician with a soldering iron and a heap of resistors and capacitors is becoming out of date in the new world of integrated circuits. Now that the silicon chip has taken over, there is less occasion to select individual components. The resistor problem has been replaced with that of identifying the individual wires making up a multicore cable. The component wires are identified by solid colours or by combinations of pairs of colours arranged as a spiral stripe. The colours are the same 12 as those used for resistor codes. Several laboratory studies have shown that colour defectives are prone to error in identifying the cables. Where it is a question of matching pairs of wires, most colour defectives will make a reasonable guess, given sufficient light. However, if the matching requirement is by name, e.g. *connect the green/orange wire to Pin 4*, there is an unacceptable risk of error. Incorrect connection of a wire may be critical for the safe operation of a system. The Clapham rail crash of 1988 was caused by a signalling fault and one possible explanation was the misinterpretation of colour coded wires in the connection to the automated system. The industry standard for employees in this sector of the telecommunications industry now includes a colour vision check.

Poor colour vision is likely to be a handicap for anyone in the electronics industry and will be a bar for some sectors. Applicants for the Modern Apprenticeship and the National Traineeship are told:

> *Those applicants with mild sensory impairment may be able to satisfy the selection criteria; however, it should be noted that colour blindness might be a barrier to fulfilling all the relevant Health and Safety Requirements.*

Many activities within the electronics and telecommunications industry do not require normal colour vision; examples are research and development or sales and marketing. Manufacture, installation and maintenance all require accurate work with devolved responsibility to the technician doing the job. A requirement for normal colour vision must be accepted.

The office

What of the world of work in general? Most jobs do not demand any critical colour judgements and there is no question of the colour-blind applicant being rejected. Nor is there any reason why colour deficiency should prove any handicap on the job. Nevertheless, difficulty in seeing colours can produce some minor problems. In the office, many filing systems are colour coded. This should have no worse effect than simply slowing down the colour deficient employee a bit; they may have to read a printed title or ask a colleague for assistance. Dealing with coloured demonstration material may be difficult. Few business meetings are now complete without a set of computer generated presentation slides. When preparing such presentations, the colour deficient employees should stick to a safe palette; most presentation software applications include a selection of tried and tested colour combinations. Problems are likely when reading multi colour graphs and charts; this is the general version of the London Underground map problem. Once there are more than four or five colours to differentiate, it is likely that someone will have problems, especially as the colours are rarely selected with the colour deficient in mind. The ease of production of multi coloured diagrams with modern software, coupled with the widespread availability of colour printers, means that every internal report is replete with coloured diagrams. If it is important for the reader to identify the lines or the pie chart sectors with the legend, the use of a coloured filter to change contrast will be found invaluable.

A newly qualified accountant of my acquaintance was employed on his first audit where he was required to check the accounts of a company to establish that they were correct. He found that the figures did not add up. There appeared to be money missing and he reported a suspected fraud to his superiors. There was threat of a major investigation, until one of his superiors checked the figures. The colour-blind accountant had not noticed that some figures were in red, which in accounting convention signifies a debit. There was no fraud. The accountancy firm was embarrassed and threatened to dismiss the colour-blind member of staff. Fortunately for him, they didn't. Now he takes the precaution of viewing the accounts through a red filter to ensure no debits have gone unnoticed. This anecdote illustrates the point that the colour-blind person learns to deal with most situations through learning by experience and knows when to take extra care. Every now and than, some unexpected colour combination is used and creates a problem.

Counter attack

The theme running through this chapter is that colour vision deficiency affects performance in many jobs. Colour defectives are barred from some occupations. It is therefore in everybody's interest that entrants be screened for colour deficiency, so that they can make appropriate career choices. There are many occupations where there is no formal ban on colour defectives, but where they are liable to perform poorly in some situations or even be potentially dangerous. With the increased awareness of colour vision deficiencies, we may expect to see more employers to employ vision screening and to reject applicants who fail the test. This chapter has emphasised the range of colour deficiency that exists. There are occupations where a mild colour defective can perform perfectly well, though a dichromat would be unsuitable. The Ishihara test is the test most commonly used and it is the most sensitive. If it is used without understanding, it is likely that suitable applicants with only a mild colour deficiency may be rejected.

If so, these rejections will be challenged. Most Western countries have some form of Disabilities Act or Human Rights Act in place, which impose duties on employers. In addition, most large employers and educational bodies operate a non-discrimination policy and consider themselves obliged to provide assistance and support to the disadvantaged as necessary. The colour-blind do not, as yet, constitute any form of pressure group, in contrast to many other forms of disability. There is no organisation for a colour-blind person to join; even the left handed are better organised.

Summary: careers

Good colour vision is a formal entry requirement for several occupations. These are usually those where a failure to respond correctly to a coloured signal or colour code could result in a life-threatening situation. Examples include the Armed Forces, transport, uniformed services and some branches of engineering. A few of these occupations offer an alternative to the Ishihara plates, usually a lantern test. This may allow those with only a mild colour vision deficiency to be passed for entry.

There are many jobs where a colour misjudgement can prove expensive; they would include the manufacture of colour articles, fabrics and carpets, or quality control in food and agriculture. Employers would be well advised to use some form of colour screening for employees, so that the colour deficient may be assigned to suitable tasks.

Chapter 8 - Techniques that may help

Congenital colour vision deficiency has no cure. It is as well to face up to this fact at the start. Nothing - whether medicine, training or special spectacles - will produce normal colour vision in a defective person. Some of the sensation and joy of colour will remain unknown. However, there are techniques that can be used to help discriminate between colours or to perform some tasks. We will start by dismissing the techniques that do not work.

Ineffective remedies

Before the physiological basis was fully understood, there was a feeling that colour vision deficiency was in some way related to mental laziness and that education and training would help the sufferer improve their abilities. Although colour vision deficiency can be a problem for farmers, it was not regarded as a serious handicap in the world of work until the growth of the transport industry and the use of coloured signal lamps. Some serious accidents on the railway system and at sea drew attention to the problem and led to the introduction of colour vision tests. The end of the nineteenth century was a good time for charlatans. Proposed cures for colour blindness included injections of cobra venom or extracts from marigolds or lobsters. A German report proposed warming one eye. Coaching in colour naming was offered for those about to apply for employment on the railways.

Many young men were disappointed in their ambition to train as pilots during World War II when they failed the colour vision test. This prompted a fresh surge of quack cures, including injections of iodine, flashing light therapy or a hefty dose of vitamins. The only effective method for a colour defective wishing to pass the screening test was to learn the correct responses to the Ishihara tests by heart, and this was indeed done. In the USA, the American Society of Ophthalmology issued a statement that there was no cure for the problem and that coaching recruits to pass colour screening test could endanger national security. Their words are still valid today:

> No method had been found for the correction of colour blindness, whether called 'color weakness', 'color confusion' or 'color defectiveness'. Men can be coached to pass tests, but their physiologic deficiency cannot be repaired. Any claims to the contrary, any treatment which convinces operators that they can see colours they could not see before will decrease safety in transportation, decrease security in national defense, and decrease efficiency in industry.

A Japanese company marketed a device in the 1960s that applied electrical stimulation to the head via electrodes fastened to the temples. Application of the device for 20 minutes a day over a year was claimed to improve colour vision. When tested in London, subjects showed no improvement and nothing has been heard of the device since.

Performance on a colour vision screening test may be improved by viewing the plate under flickering illumination. Apparently, a flicker frequency of about 2 cycles per second is most effective. Some colour defectives find blinking rapidly improves their vision somewhat. There have been proposals to construct a device to exploit this effect. A rotating disc would be mounted on a spectacle frame, powered by a miniature electric motor. The aperture in the disc is sized to block vision for one quarter of each rotation, so producing the required flickering effect. I can find no record of the device being evaluated in practice.

Filters

Try this simple demonstration. Draw a green line and a red line on a piece of paper and look at them through a piece of red glass or plastic. If you can't find red and green pens, use a map of the London Underground or any suitable picture in this book. Seen through the red glass, the green line goes black and the red line almost disappears. This happens whatever sort of colour vision deficiency you may or may not have. If your deficiency results in the lines looking the same when seen without any filter, they now look different and can be told apart. Looking at the world through rose coloured spectacles does enable the colour defective to tell colours apart that were otherwise indistinguishable. First, a look at what sorts of colour filter there are.

Most coloured filters work by absorbing some components of the light passing through them. There are some specialised filters that operate by reflecting components of the spectrum and transmitting the rest. The net result is the same; some wavelengths are transmitted more than others. If the filter scatters the light so that it emerges in all directions it is said to be translucent or diffuse; it is not possible to see a clear image when looking though a diffuse filter. We are only interested in transparent filters, where the light goes straight through and an undistorted image may be seen when looking through the filter.

When white light, containing all the wavelengths of the spectrum, passes through a coloured filter, some wavelengths are absorbed more than others and the emergent light looks coloured. We speak of a red or a green filter, according to the appearance of the light it transmits. However, the eye interprets a mixture of wavelengths as a single colour, so that the appearance of a filter is an inadequate guide to what colours are actually being transmitted. The only way to specify the performance of a filter accurately is to give its spectral transmittance curve. An example is shown in **Figure 35** of the transmission curves of three types of yellow filter. All of them would look the same to the eye when illuminated by white light. The common yellow filter has a low transmittance for blue light, but transmits wavelengths from green to red, which, as we know, combine in the eye to give a sensation of yellow. This sort of filter is inexpensive and would be used for stage lighting and such work. If it is desired to pass yellow light alone,

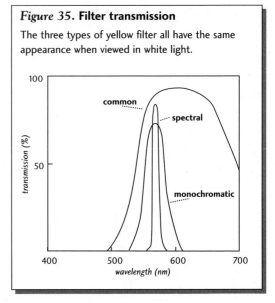

Figure 35. **Filter transmission**

The three types of yellow filter all have the same appearance when viewed in white light.

then the transmittance curve must be narrower and the filter is now described as a spectral filter. An even narrower pass band would deserve the name monochromatic. The common yellow filter and the monochromatic filter shown in the figure would appear to have the same hue when a white light source is viewed through them. However, the spectral filter absorbs a much larger proportion of the light energy and so would appear darker.

Although the various yellow filters appear the same colour in white light, in other circumstances they behave quite differently. Imagine viewing a red light source though the filters in succession; here, the red source contains only red wavelengths. The red light passes happily through the common yellow filter and is seen as red. However, the spectral filter does not pass any red light and so appears black. Colour filters are produced for many specialised purposes, in photography, colour printing and scientific applications. The more exacting the task, the more precisely is the spectral transmission curve defined and the more expensive the filter.

Filters for red-green deficiencies

Look again at Figure 17, which shows lines of confusion for red-blind and green-blind colour defectives on the chromaticity diagram. When considering the use of filters for colour defectives, it can be helpful to group the confusions into three classes

- Both red and green-blind persons confuse colours along the top right hand edge of the spectral envelope, i.e. from about 530 nm (green) to 700 nm (red) - if indeed they can see that far into the deep red end of the spectrum.

- Red-blind persons confuse the range of purples along the bottom of the diagram, while green-blind persons will confuse a purple with the blue that lies on the same confusion line.

- Both red and green-blind persons can confuse grey with a bluish-green - though not quite the same one as each other.

Those who are red or green colour weak will display similar confusions, but not so severely.

Looking at the world though a coloured filter can help the colour defective discriminate between pairs of colours that would otherwise look the same. A filter can modify all three attributes of a colour:

- Hue. In the real world, virtually all coloured objects and lights reflect or emit a mixture of several wavelengths, which are seen by the eye as a single hue. About the only monochromatic colour in everyday life is provided by a sodium street light. A purple object reflects both blue and red light. If it is viewed though a red filter, the filter obstructs the blue light and the object now appears red. Both the lights reflected from a coloured object and the transmission curve of a filter may have a complicated spectral distribution. As a result, the hue shift observed when looking through a filter may be unexpected. It is therefore impossible to predict what a "green" object will look like when viewed through a "yellow" filter without knowing the spectral distribution of both.

- Lightness. Since a filter only absorbs light, it cannot increase the absolute brightness of a colour. However, the eye deals largely in relativities and contrasts. If red flowers among green leaves are viewed though a red filter, the red flowers will appear to increase in brightness against a background of darkened leaves.

- Saturation. By absorbing the desaturating components in a mix of wavelengths, a filter can enhance a colour's saturation, e.g. a blue filter absorbs green, yellow and red. A desaturated blue colour viewed through it would appear more saturated. What has happened is that a mix of colours that together make white have been removed. The result is that the blue looks stronger.

Viewing a scene though a coloured filter can help a colour defective in two main ways:

- lightness changes as the scene is viewed with and without a filter
- colour changes, when the scene is viewed continuously though a filter

By looking at a scene though red and green filters in succession, a red-green defective can make deductions as to the nature of the colours. The precise change will depend on the transmission curve of the filter, the spectral distribution of the light from the coloured object and the nature of the colour deficiency. *Table 19* shows the changes that can be expected. If a colour defective is to use this method for colour identification, practice will be necessary, preferably helped by a colour normal who can say what the colours really are. In practice, the main use of a colour filter is to discriminate between colours that otherwise look the same. This is of great practical use in identifying colour codes in maps and diagrams. Remember it is the change in brightness that helps; permanent viewing though a colour filter would simply create a fresh set of confusions. For instance, viewing though a red filter results in red lettering on a white background becoming invisible. A red-blind person will find a red filter invaluable for differentiating between the Bakerloo and Central lines on the Underground map, which are otherwise indistinguishable. However, the red filter now makes the Central and Hammersmith lines look the same, which were previously different.

Table 19. Brightness changes observed when colours are viewed first though a red and then through a green filter.

Class of confusion	Colour viewed	Brightness change
1 (red-green)	red yellow green	darker no change brighter
2 (purples)	reddish-purple bluish-purple	darker lighter
3 (grey-cyan)	grey blue-green	no change brighter

Coloured lenses

The previous section described the use of filters to help discriminate between colours that otherwise look the same. The user needs to carry one or two filters and use them when needed for tasks such as map reading. Another possibility is to wear a pair of tinted spectacles. Now the filter is used to enhance the appearance of the world in such a way that colours look brighter and some discriminations are improved. There is no universally successful recipe for the choice of filter characteristic. There are several reports of colour deficient individuals who have found this to be helpful and who choose to wear tinted spectacles permanently. A green-weak butcher attended the City University clinic in London and after some trials was prescribed a magenta pair of spectacles. He expressed great satisfaction "*I have seen things that I knew existed but could not see before, e.g. traces of blood in veins...poultry showing green blemishes and slight marks on poultry caused by fat...I can see different shades of green in trees and grass...clouds are no longer grey*". After one year, he was still wearing the tinted lenses, including for driving.

In as far as it is possible to generalise, tinted spectacles have been found most likely to be of benefit to green-weak colour defectives and may well benefit red-weak individuals. A dichromat, whether red or green-blind, is unlikely to experience much benefit from the continuous wearing of tinted spectacles. The appearance of the world will change when wearing the glasses, but new confusions will replace the pre-existing ones. Prescription of the optimum tint needs to be by an experienced practitioner who has access to a range of filters. The best tint is established, first by trials in the clinic and then by wearing the filters for a few days. Once the tint has been selected, it is possible to dye polycarbonate (CR39) prescription lenses with the exact colour required.
The idea of using tinted spectacles is not new. First proposed in the 1830s, the idea was revived by the great physicist Maxwell:

> By furnishing Mr X with a red and a green glass, which he could distinguish only by their shape, I enabled him to make judgements in previously doubtful cases of a colour with perfect certainty. I have since had a pair of spectacles constructed with one eye glass red and the other green. These Mr X tends to use for a length of time, and he hopes to acquire the habit of discriminating red from green tints by their different effects on the two eyes. Though he can never acquire our sensation of red, he may discern for himself what things are red, and the mental process may become so familiar to him as to act unconsciously like a new sense.

Maxwell's proposal of the wearing of different filters over the two eyes anticipated the development during the 1940s of monocular colour correction filters such as the X-Chrom lens. These are described in a later section.

At the time of writing, evaluation is under way of the prospect of using a notch filter to improve colour discrimination in those with a weak form of colour deficiency. People with the anomalous form of colour vision defect have three sets of colour receptor, but the response of the red and green receptors is much closer together than is should be. See Figure 18. Now, suppose the world is viewed through a filter that absorbs light in the region where the two curves overlap. The difference in response of the two types of cone will be artificially increased and the eye will be better able to differentiate between colours that are otherwise easily confused. If it works, this technique will only be of benefit to those with the weak form of colour deficiency; it would be of no help at all to dichromats.

Filter selection

Anyone suffering from colour vision deficiency should get hold of some coloured filters and try them out. The changed appearance of the world and the way in which apparently identical colours suddenly spring apart when viewed though a filter can be quite surprising. Where filters are being used as a tool to aid colour discrimination, the choice of filter is not too critical and a first step is to try with whatever is available. A pair of red and green 3D glasses makes a good start. A simple red filter is adequate for much of the time, but is best complemented by a green or cyan filter. A cyan filter, passing green and blue light, is the complement of red. Since red-green defectives respond normally to blue, it is as well to use a cyan filter, which does not interfere with the blue colours. Thus any brightness changes observed when the cyan filter is used are due to the absorption of red light. For the same reason, a magenta filter may be preferable to a red filter, since it also passes blue light.

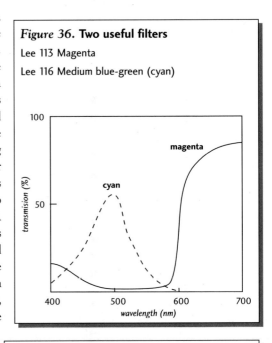

Figure 36. Two useful filters

Lee 113 Magenta

Lee 116 Medium blue-green (cyan)

Table 20. **Filter selection**

	Lee filters	Kodak Wratten
Red	Primary red 106 Light red 182	
Green	Primary green 139	
Cyan	Medium blue- green 116	
Magenta	Lavender 058 Magenta 113 Bright pink 128	Wratten 32

The most widely available filters with a range of defined characteristics are sold for theatrical lighting. Lee Filters make a wide range of filters, including several suitable for colour defectives. **Figure 36** shows the transmission curves of cyan and magenta filters; this pair of colours should be the first two colours to try by anyone wishing for help with colour discrimination. **Table 20** gives a list of other filters that may be found helpful. For general purposes, the selection is not critical.

Monocular correction

The colour normal sees the full range of colours because the brain can combine the responses from the red, green and blue photoreceptors into a coloured picture. The photoreceptors each can respond to quite a wide range of wavelengths - the red receptor responds to most green wavelengths, and the green receptor responds to most red, except the longest wavelengths. It is therefore possible to devise a filter that could turn a green-blind person into a pretty passable imitation of a red-blind defective. Using a green filter would reduce the eye's sensitivity to red and shape the response curve to mimic that of a red-blind defective. At first sight, there would seem to be little point in replacing one sort of deficiency with another. Now suppose this filter is placed over one eye only. The brain now gets the full set of red, green and blue signals; blue and green come from one eye and blue and red from the other. The brain now has all the information it needs to see in full colour: can it use it?

It turns out that using a filter over one eye can produce an improvement in colour discrimination. Such a filter is sometimes described as haploscopic. The images produced by the two eyes now have a different pattern of brightness. Psychologists use the term binocular rivalry to describe the perceptual problems produced when the brain has to deal with different images produced by the two eyes. If the images produced by the two eyes differ too much from each other, the non-dominant image may simply be suppressed and ignored. Where both eyes see the same image, but with differences in brightness, a phenomenon known as lustre occurs. Objects appear to glitter or have an iridescent appearance and this contributes to the enthusiastic reaction of some users, who report that colours are now seen to have a special brightness. This leaves the question whether there is objective evidence of improved colour vision. As always, it is difficult to generalise because of the range of red-green defects found in the general population, but as a crude statement, wearing a monocular contact lens can

- improve performance on the Ishihara test
- fail to improve the results of lantern tests

- increase and change the errors on the FM100 test

- change the results on the D15 test unpredictably

These results cannot be said to demonstrate any objective improvement in colour vision. The ability to pass the Ishihara test while wearing a colour correction filter says nothing about colour vision, other than that testers should ensure that the subject does not wear correction when taking the test.

This is the principle behind the use of a coloured contact lens fitted to one eye only. While the idea had been around for a long time, the first widespread commercial application was in the USA, where the X-Chrom lens was introduced in the early 1970s. This was a dyed plastic contact lens, transmitting red light beyond 575 nm, with some low (10% or less) transmission below 480 nm. The lens is worn in the non-dominant eye. This ensures maximum acuity from the unobstructed dominant eye, with additional colour and depth information being fed from the other eye. Perhaps surprisingly, only one type of lens was available, for both red and green defectives. The optical density of the lens could be chosen to suit individuals. The lens produces both brightness changes and colour changes as described above. Other makes of lens are now available, which will be described below.

Wearing a colour filter over one eye may have unexpected effects on depth perception. The effect is known as the Pulfrich pendulum. It is often quoted as a potential problem, even danger, which may be associated with the wearing of a single corrective lens, and is therefore described here. Make a pendulum about a meter or more long out of a piece of string and a suitable weight. Set it swinging in a straight line so that it swings across your line of sight. Look at it with both eyes, but with one eye covered with a dark glass, such as the lens from a pair of dark sunglasses. Remarkably, the pendulum now appears to be swinging in an ellipse. Reducing the light to one eye

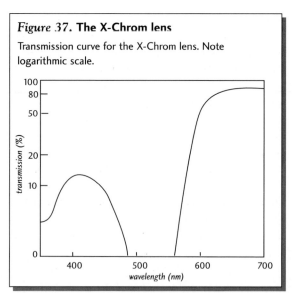

Figure 37. The X-Chrom lens

Transmission curve for the X-Chrom lens. Note logarithmic scale.

has slowed that eye down and it takes longer for the retina to gather the visual information about the position of the bob and send it to the brain. The two eyes therefore see the swinging bob in different positions: one where it is now and the other where it was a fraction of a second ago. The result is that the brain perceives motion in an ellipse. It seems unlikely that this would be a problem in practice. The filters used for colour vision correction are probably not dense enough to produce the illusion. At any rate, no problems of this nature have been reported. The Pulfrich effect on depth perception only occurs when looking at moving objects and the illusion would be reduced in real situations by the presence of surrounding objects.

Commercial products

There are two major brands of coloured lens produced: the ChromaGen lens in Britain and the ColorMax in North America. Both have been approved in the USA by the Food and Drug Administration (FDA), and this approval is featured in their marketing. However, the approval indicates only that the lenses are safe for use and the FDA neither endorses nor criticises the claims made concerning colour correction.

ColorMax
"See a spring garden in its full glory! Enjoy Claude Monet's famous Water Lilies painting"
The ColorMax lenses are tinted lenses, designed to be worn over both eyes as a pair of tinted sunglasses. ColorMax lenses are available in two classifications, to suit protan and deutan colour vision deficiencies. Each of these is available in five levels of attenuation, making ten lenses in all. After a colour vision diagnosis, the patient is given a selected lens for evaluation, wearing it in a trial spectacle frame. ColorMax lenses are claimed to be suitable for dichromats as well as those suffering the weak form of red-green colour blindness. When a tint is found satisfactory, the lenses can be made up in the user's prescription.

The general comments on the permanent wearing of colour filters that were made above will apply to the ColorMax lenses. Discrimination between some colours that were previously confused will be improved, but at the cost of introducing some new confusions. The world may well appear more colourful and users enjoy the altered view. Performance on some colour vision tests may be enhanced. This does not indicate improved colour vision and most tests taken for occupational requirements specifically require that corrective lenses are not worn during the test.

The company's web site contains testimonials from enthusiastic users:

"My experience with ColorMax® Lenses has been outstanding! I couldn't believe my eyes when I could see the changes in the colours…! These lenses will make life so much easier; I recommend them to anyone with a color vision deficiency".

ChromaGen

The ChromaGen lens was developed in the United Kingdom in the early 1990s by David Harris. It has attracted considerable publicity and was chosen as a Millennium Product to represent British design. The lens is available in 8 hues, with a range of densities and diameters. The contact lens has a tinted pupil, with the rest of the lens clear. Since the tinted region of the lens sits over the black pupil of the eye, the coloured tint is not obvious to anyone else. In most cases, the tinted lens is worn in one eye only, but some patients obtain a benefit by having different tints over each eye. At the start, it was felt by the developers that tinted spectacles would not be acceptable, since the use of a pair of spectacles where only one lens was coloured would produce a somewhat bizarre appearance. However, the use of a partially reflecting coating on the surface of the spectacle lens effectively disguises the coloured tint underneath, and Chromagen spectacles are now available with the appearance to the onlooker of a conventional pair of mirror sunglasses.

The lens must be fitted by a trained practitioner. A preliminary colour vision assessment is made using Ishihara plates. The most suitable tinted lens for the patient is then selected by trial. A standard brightly coloured target is used, which is presented either as a computer image or a back lit transparency. The patient views the image while the practitioner holds a trial filter over the non-dominant eye. The patient views the colour image for a few seconds and is asked for a response. The following are regarded as positive responses

- increased brightness in the colours

- more coloured bands visible in the target image

- fluorescence of some colours

The practitioner goes through all the lenses one by one; the best lens may be selected by making forced choices among those producing a favourable response. When the best lens has been chosen for the non-dominant eye, the other lenses are then tried over the dominant eye. For some patients an improvement is found by wearing different tints over the two eyes.

The patient then wears the selected spectacles for a period of at least an hour and is encouraged to view a wide range of coloured scenes. A visit to a local garden centre has been found ideal to give patients a feeling for the novel experience of the colour enhancing lenses. After this time, the patient is interviewed and asked about their experience of wearing the lenses. If the patient is satisfied and wishes to purchase, the lenses are then dispensed. It is possible for the lenses to be made up to the wearer's prescription. Some prefer to wear non-corrective plano contact lenses in combination with their usual spectacles.

The makers of the ChromaGen lens asked patients for their assessment of the effectiveness of the lens, both on the day of fitting and three months later. The main question was: Please give a score of 0 to 10 for the overall improvement in your colour vision (0=no improvement, 5=significant improvement, 10=dramatic improvement). On the day of fitting, the average rating for subjective improvement was 7.15, with 97% scoring 5 or above. About one quarter of the patients returned the questionnaire after three months use of the lens. Results were still good, with a mean improvement rating of 6.1. Only 4% had discontinued use, with 39% wearing the lens every day. Patients found the lens useful to wear at work, and several stated that the lens had helped them get a job or stay in the one they had.

While not everyone takes to the lens, many wearers are enthusiastic. *"It was a completely novel experience for me. Not only can I see red fully now but everything else is brighter. Without it everything looks very drab"*.

Availability
Over the last hundred years and more there have been several attempts to produce and market aids to colour vision correction. Some have been shown to assist the colour deficient in discriminating between colours that would otherwise be confused and many wearers have responded enthusiastically. However, no product has established itself over the long term and at the time of writing the ColorMax lens has been withdrawn from the market.

Driving

There have been several proposals for special spectacles specifically designed to help car drivers with colour defects. Most of the designs involved the use of red or green filter strips - sometimes both. The strips were mounted either at the top or side of the lens, which was otherwise clear. The driver therefore looks through the uncoloured centre of the lens for normal driving, but can check the colour of a signal by moving the head to look through the coloured filter. These spectacles have never become widely used and would not seem to have much value in practice. Problems in driving come from the failure to notice coloured signals, whether stop lights or traffic lights, in an often confusing background of coloured street lights and advertisements. Once the light has been seen, there is seldom a problem in deciding what it is.

There was a fashion during the 1950s for night driving glasses. They were tinted amber and it was claimed that they cut dazzle from oncoming headlights. Experiments showed them to have little or no value and colour defectives were sternly warned against using them:

> *Yellow tinted glasses are particularly dangerous to colour defectives. Such people, who are likely to seize upon any device which may help them, have a reduced sensitivity to light, so that even the palest filter will have a marked effect on their night vision.*

The makers of the ColorMax lenses specifically advise against wearing the lens when driving, especially at night. The general problems of colour deficiency and driving were discussed fully in Chapter 8. The would seem to be few, if any, advantages in wearing corrective lenses for driving, and some real disadvantages.

User experience

There is a fairly extensive research literature on the wearing of colour enhancing lenses. Reviewing the literature produces a rather downbeat view of their effectiveness. This may be because academic researchers have high standards of proof and are asking the question whether the lenses *really* improve colour vision. The answer to this question must be no: it is impossible for a colour-blind person to experience the true sensation of colour that is so important to artists and designers. However, the lenses certainly can improve discrimination among colours that would otherwise be confused, and the lustre effect gives a brightness to colours that was absent before.

Wearers may need to learn colour names afresh. The average colour defective learns to use all sorts of cues, especially brightness, to improve the success rate when guessing the name of a colour. The new wearer is likely to make mistakes when naming colours; this is not an indication that the lens is not effective.

The response of users, admittedly filtered though the lens manufacturers, is often enthusiastic. Use of the lens has enhanced the ability of many to follow their hobbies;

examples given include bird watchers, stamp collectors and artists. Many people in jobs that require some degree of colour judgement have found their performance improved. Electricians, photographers, painters and decorators come into this category. A word of caution is necessary here. It would be most unwise, and potentially dangerous, for a person to obtain a job with the help of a colour enhancing lens from which he would otherwise be excluded.

Summary: techniques

The use of coloured filters can be of great value to a colour defective. Most of the experience in their use relates to red-green colour defectives and the applications may be summarised:

Hand held filters. Using a red or a pair of red and green filters can be very useful in identifying colours or discriminating between pairs of colours that otherwise look the same. Such activities as map reading, using multi colour legends in diagrams or even using the London Underground map are greatly assisted. The target is viewed with and without the filters and the brightness changes are noted.

Tinted spectacles. Wearing a pair of tinted lenses over both eyes can make the world seem more colourful and aid discrimination between colours that would normally be confused. Maximum benefits are obtained with red or green-weak colour defectives; dichromats will show less benefit. A range of lenses is available, allowing the individual to select the tint of preference. Caution in use is required: the tinted lenses may introduce new and unexpected colour confusions and their use while driving, especially at night, may worsen performance.

Monocular contact lenses. A tinted contact lens worn in one eye only provides more colour information to the brain and allows colours to be discriminated that would other wise be confused. Some coloured objects take on a lustrous appearance, which increases the subjective feeling that the world now looks more brightly coloured. The use of such a lens cannot recreate true normal colour vision, but many users are enthusiastic with the improvement in their sight. Use of a single lens may affect depth perception of moving objects, particularly in low light levels.

All the aids can improve performance on some tests for colour vision deficiencies. This should not be regarded as a satisfactory pass for entry into any vocation that requires good colour vision.

Bibliography

Many journals and books were consulted during the course of writing. Up-to-date information on research developments is to be found mainly in the pages of conference proceedings or academic journals. These are often difficult to get hold of outside a university library and a full list has not been given. A selection is given here of suggested further reading. The recent surveys contain extensive bibliographies and would provide a good starting point for anyone wishing to explore the subject further. The World Wide Web is increasingly a source of information, especially where commercial products are involved. URLs of useful web sites are listed along with more conventional references. Web sites suffer from impermanence and some may have disappeared. The Colour Group of Great Britain and the International Colour Vision Society websites both contain valuable links to other sites.

General

Fletcher, R. and Voke, J. **Defective colour vision: fundamentals, diagnosis and management**, Bristol: Adam Hilger, 1985. This is without doubt the most comprehensive treatment of colour vision deficiency. The book is still in print, but does not include recent discoveries in genetics.

Colour: Art and Science, edited by Lamb, T. and Bourria, J., Cambridge University Press, 1995 is a collection of the Darwin College Lectures given in Cambridge by experts in the field and deals with many of the themes touched on in this book.

An up to date and technical treatment of colour vision is to be found in

Gegenfurtner, K.R. and Sharpe, L.T. **Color Vision: From Genes to Perception**, Cambridge University Press, 1999.

An undergraduate level text on the visual system is available at
http://www.webvision.med.utah.edu/

The Colour Group of Great Britain is a multidisciplinary group of people interested in all aspects of colour. More information is to be found on its web site.
http://www.city.ac.uk/colourgroup/

The International Colour Vision Society has a web site at
http://orlab.optom.unsw.edu.au/ICVS/

Chapter 1. Light and colour

There are many text books dealing with light and colour from a physical point of view. Any good school text book should cover the ground.
Sobel, M.I. **Light,** University of Chicago Press, 1989 is a wide ranging treatment of light and vision.

Chapter 2. Colour vision

Gregory, R.L. **Eye and brain: the psychology of seeing,** London: Oxford University Press, 1997. The updated version of Gregory's classic book gives an excellent overview of visual perception.

Armstrong, T. **Colour Perception: A practical approach to colour theory,** Diss: Tarquin Publications, 1991 is a cheap and enjoyable introduction to colour theory. It includes many practical demonstrations.

Chapter 3. Colour vision deficiencies

The general subject of CVD is well covered in the book by Fletcher and Voke. For recent developments in genetics, read the papers by Nathan and by Neitz et al., plus the chapter by Sharpe et. al.

Nathan, J. **The genes for colour vision.** Scientific American 260(2):29-35, 1989.

Neitz, J., Neitz, M., and Kainz, P.M. **Visual pigment gene structure and the severity of color vision defects.** Science 274:801-804, 1996.

Neitz, M. and Neitz, J. **Molecular genetics of color vision and color vision defects.** Arch Ophthalmol 118(May):691-700, 2000.

Sharpe, L.T., Stockman, A., Jaegle, H., and Nathans, J. **Opsin genes, cone photopigments, color vision and color blindness.** In: **Color vision: from genes to perception,** edited by Gengenfurter, K.R. and Sharpe, L.T., Cambridge: Cambridge University Press, 1999,p. 3-52.

This book has only touched on the rare complaint of achromatopsia. For more information visit the achromatopsia network
http://www.achromat.org

Chapter 4. Diagnosis

The various tests for diagnosing colour vision deficiency are well covered in the book by Jennifer Birch of the City University, which also gives a good general account of colour vision deficiency.

Birch, J. **Diagnosis of defective colour vision**, Oxford: Butterworth Heinemann, 2001. Mrs Birch works at The Department of Optometry and Visual Science at the City University, London EC1V 7DD, which is a leading centre of colour vision testing.

Many examples of colour vision tests are to be found on the web. Try:
http://www.umds.ac.uk/physiology/daveb/brainday/colourblindness/cblind.htm
http://members.aol.com/nocolorvsn/color.htm
http://www.high-tower.com/products/paper-col/ishihara_test.html

Chapter 5. Appearance of colours

Brettel, H., Vienot, F., and Mollon, J.D. **Computerised simulation of colour appearance for dichromats**. Journal of the Optical Society of America 14(10):2647-2655, 1997. This paper sets out the theoretical basis for the transformation of images to simulate dichromatic vision.

Most development of techniques to simulate colour deficient vision has been based on computer images destined for the web.

Rigden, C. **The eye of the beholder. Designing for colour-blind users.** British Telecommunications Engineering 17(January):2-6, 1999 provides a good introduction.

The following web sites have good examples.
Safe web for colour-deficient vision, from British Telecom
http://innovate.bt.com/people/rigdence/colours/

http://www.colorfield.com/ The Colorfield Digital Media site shows examples of transformations produced by its commercial software Colorfield Insight

http://www.visibone.com/ A series of aids to designing in Websafe colours, including examples of colour -blind simulations, is to be found at the Visibone site

Chapter 6. Everyday Life

The research paper by Cole and Stewart remains one of the best sources of information on this topic. Steward, J.M. and Cole, B.L. **What do colour defectives say about every day tasks?** Optometry and Visual Science 66(5):288-295, 1989.

Rosenthal, O. and Phillips, R.H. **Coping with Color-Blindness**, New York:Avery Publishing Group, 1997 treats this topic at length, but the statements made in the book are often at variance with conventional opinion.

Trevor-Roper, P. **The world through blunted sight**, London: Penguin Books, 1990 is a classic book that looks at the relation between visual defects and art.

The same topic is treated by the French author, Philippe Lanthony, who has done much research on colour-blind painters. Lanthony, P. **Les yeux des peintres**, Paris:L'age d'Homme, 1999.

Chapter 7. Careers

Careers advisory services carry lists of occupations where CVD may be a barrier to entry. If in doubt, write to the regulatory body concerned with the occupation of interest. Rules change and it may be that a mild defect is not a handicap. Spalding gives an excellent account of the difficulties faced by colour deficient doctors.

HSE Colour Vision. Guidance Note MS7, HSE Books, 1987.
Spalding, J.A.B. **Colour vision deficiency in the medical profession**. British Journal of General Practice 49(June):469-475, 1999.

Chapter 8. Techniques that may help

The American FDA has issued a statement on the use of corrective filters. Otherwise it is difficult to get impartial advice. Lens manufacturers run their own web sites. The Chromagen lens is manufactured by Cantor and Nissel, who give a list of licensed opticians who prescribe the lens.
http://www.cantor-nissel.co.uk/chromg.htm

The most readily available colour filters are those sold for theatrical lighting. Look in the Yellow Pages under Theatrical Suppliers. Lee Filters provides a comprehensive list of filters with technical data on their website.
http://www.leefilters.com/

Acknowledgements

This book is based entirely on the work of others and owes its existence to the many scientists, from John Dalton on, who have observed, theorised and investigated the phenomena of colour vision and its deficiencies. Major references are given in the bibliography and the interested reader can use these as a starting point for further reading. I have been helped by many people while writing this book. Meetings of the Colour Group of Great Britain provided stimulating presentations and the opportunity to meet many active researchers. Professor Arnold Wilkins of the University of Essex , Christine Rigden of BTexact Technologies and Dr Anthony Spalding read the manuscript and offered helpful suggestions for improvement. Professor Lindsey Sharpe of the University of Newcastle prepared some of the computer transformations and resolved some genetic queries. Dr Philippe Lanthony of the Centre Hospitalier National d'Ophtalmologie des Quinze-Vingts shared his research into colour vision deficiency and the visual arts. Dr David Harris demonstrated his Chromagen diagnostic procedure to me and Adrian Chorley of the CAA updated the section on visual requirements for pilots. Professor Jay Neitz of the Medical College of Wisconsin provided details on the new genetic test for colour vision deficiency.

Picture credits

Figures 4 and 14	The Colour Group of Great Britain
Figure 6	Britannica® DVD2000 © 1994-2000 Encyclopedia Britannica, Inc
Figure 12	Petra Stoerig, Wavelength information processing vs colour perception: evidence from blindsight and colour blind sight. In *Colour Vision*, Walter de Gruyter, Berlin 1998, pp131-147. Reproduced by kind permission of Walter de Gruyter Gmbh.
Figures 13, 26 and 32	Professor L T Sharpe, University of Newcastle
Figure 22	Ishihara's Test for Colour Deficiency. Reproduced by permission ©Isshinkai Foundation, published by Kanehara Trading Co.
Figure 24	D G Colour Ltd, Salisbury
Figure 28	Sussex Vision, Lancing
Figure 29	Visibone
Figure 31	©Transport for London. Reproduced by kind permission of London's Transport Museum
Figure 33	Colorfield Digital Media

Cover photographs prepared using Colorfield™ Insight software

Main Index